Founded
on the

Rock

Finding God's Order for Your Family

by

Ray Llarena

Founded on the Rock
Copyright © 1994, 1998, 2019 — Ray Llarena
ALL RIGHTS RESERVED

This book was originally published under the title, *Setting Your House in Order*. The text has been revised and totally re-typeset in a new, easy-reading format.

All biblical quotations are taken from the King James Version of the Bible, unless otherwise noted. References marked NKJV are from the New King James Version of the Bible © copyright 1979, 1980, 1982 by Thomas Nelson, Inc., Nashville, Tennessee. References marked NIV are from the New International Version of the Bible, copyright 1973, 1978, 1984 by International Bible Society.

McDougal Publishing is a ministry of The McDougal Foundation, Inc., a Maryland nonprofit corporation dedicated to spreading the Gospel of the Lord Jesus Christ to as many people as possible in the shortest time possible.

Published by:

McDougal Publishing
P.O. Box 3595
Hagerstown, MD 21742-3595

Visit our website: www.mcdougal.org

ISBN 978-1-884369-91-9
(Formerly 1-884369-02-2)

Printed in the U.S., the U.K. and Australia
For Worldwide Distribution

DEDICATION

This book is dedicated:

To the Lord Jesus Christ, the Foundation and Head of every family.

To my three beautiful children—Joy, David, and Leah—whom I love very much and hold close to my heart. They are my most precious treasure in life.

To the memory of my loving wife, who has now gone to be with the Lord, but who patiently and faithfully walked with me through the struggles of life for nineteen years.

> *Through wisdom is an house builded; and by understanding it is established: and by knowledge shall the chambers be filled with all precious and pleasant riches.*
>
> Proverbs 24:3-4

Contents

Introduction 7

Part I: Understanding God's Purposes 13
1. God's Purpose for the Individual 15
2. God's Purpose for Marriage and the Family 25
3. The Importance of a Strong Foundation 43

Part II: Building a Strong Foundation for Your Home ... 53
4. The Foundation of Agreement 55
5. The Foundation of Unity 64
6. The Foundation of Love 91

Part III: Building Upon Your Foundation 115
7. Commitment 117
8. Contentment 132
9. Consistency 150

Part IV: Special Biblical Advice 173
10. Advice to Singles 175

11. Advice to Ministers 191
12. Advice to the Unsaved 202
13. Advice to Believers Who Have Unsaved
    Spouses.. 215

Part V: Conclusion 201
14. The Power of Prayer to Change Your Situation
    and My Prayer for You 217

INTRODUCTION

Except the LORD build the house, they labour in vain that build it: except the LORD keep the city, the watchman waketh but in vain.

Psalm 127:1

It is clear to me that the problems we are experiencing in our marriages and with our children in these closing days of the twentieth century are a result of our leaving God out of our lives. God is the Author of life itself. He is the Founder of marriage as an institution and the initial Planner of the family structure. Nobody knows better how to run the household than our loving heavenly Father. Why have we shut Him out?

The result of our shutting God out is chaos. Our marriages are being destroyed in record numbers. Our children are in the streets, alienated from their parents and searching for something, they don't even know what. And our moral authority in the community is eroded as a result. I am sure this picture breaks your heart as much as it does mine.

What can we do to change it? To me, the answer is very simple. It is time to set our houses in order by returning to God's initial purpose for our lives and by obeying His Word in regard to the structure of the family and the manner in which it must be governed.

Your *"house,"* your *"city,"* is your realm of influence, your own household. God has placed you over your household as a watchman, a protector, a provider. If you are trying to govern your household or build your house without the Lord and His principles, you are laboring in vain, for it cannot be done. If you are attempting to keep your city without the Lord's presence and favor upon you, you are doomed to fail, for we simply cannot do it on our own.

I was privileged to be married for nineteen years before my darling wife passed on to Glory. Together we raised three children, of whom I am very proud because they are all serving the Lord despite the peer pressure they faced growing up, first as children and then as teenagers. The strong foundation laid for them early in life brought them through to obedience to the call of God.

I would not like to pretend that the lessons I want to put forth in this book always came easily to me. They didn't. I learned them in several ways:

- By reading the Word of God
- Through revelations that God has given me at moments of need in my own life
- Through the experiences I have had as a husband and a father
- Through what I have heard troubled people say in my years of marriage and family counseling

We are not fooled as to who the real enemy of the family is. Satan, God's enemy, delights in destroying the children whom God loves so much. Jesus clearly spoke of Satan's purpose.

The thief cometh not, but for to steal, and to kill, and to destroy: I am come that they might have life, and that they might have it more abundantly.
John 10:10

One of his most powerful techniques that Satan uses these days is to attack the family. He is destroying homes because he knows that the home is the basic element of the foundation of the Church.

Armed with this knowledge, we can turn to God and receive His help in putting the enemy to flight.

It takes great wisdom to deal with the complex issues of the modern family, but that wisdom is available to us in the Lord. He said:

> *If any of you lack wisdom, let him ask of God, that giveth to all men liberally, and upbraideth not; and it shall be given him.* James 1:5

God can give us wisdom to answer such questions as:

- What should we do when we find ourselves shouting at each other and seemingly ready to kill each other?
- What is the proper reaction if my spouse insults me?
- What should I do if I feel that my husband is taking me for granted?
- What should I do if I sense that my wife is feeling insecure about our relationship?
- How do I deal with the fact that my wife does not submit to me?
- What should I do when my children seem to have lost respect for me and I notice that they are becoming wayward or turning to worldliness?

- What should I do when my wife is angry with me? Do I need to show anger also, to get even?
- How can we maintain a romantic atmosphere in our marriage?

These are some of the questions that we are dealing with every day, and God has the answers to them. Let us submit to His Word, for unless your house is designed by the Master Architect, unless your foundations are placed by the Master Builder, and unless your finish work is done by the Master Carpenter, you are building in vain. Your house will not stand.

When we follow the principles of God's Word, when the wife finds her proper place in the home, when the husband exercises the government laid upon him by the Lord and stands as the priest over his family, and the children follow his lead, we cannot help but receive the blessings of the Lord.

When you act upon God's Word, when you step out from your limited resources into the grace of God, when you step out of your frustration into the abundance of the patience of God, you will discover the unlimited, divine resources available to you.

Let us make this discovery together as you open your heart to the message of God's Word and begin finding God's order for your family.

Pastor Ray Llarena
Chicago, Illinois

Therefore whoever hears these sayings of Mine, and does them, I will liken him to a wise man who built his house on the rock: and the rain descended, the floods came, and the winds blew and beat on that house; and it did not fall, for it was FOUNDED ON THE ROCK. *But everyone who hears these sayings of Mine, and does not do them, will be like a foolish man who built his house on the sand: and the rain descended, the floods came, and the winds blew and beat on that house; and it fell. And great was its fall.*
Matthew 7:24-27, NKJV

Part I

Understanding God's Purposes

Chapter 1

God's Purpose for the Individual

In whom also we have obtained an inheritance, being predestinated according to the purpose of him who worketh all things after the counsel of his own will: Ephesians 1:11

God is a God of purpose. He has a purpose in everything that He does. He has never done anything without a divine and eternal purpose, and He never will.

When God created the world, He had a divine purpose in mind. Creation was not an accidental collision of atoms. It was a determined act of a loving and purposeful God. And everything that God did was deemed to be *"good."*

When God separated the night from the day, He had a divine purpose in doing it. When He caused the Earth to bring forth plants and the sea to bring forth new forms of life, it was not a haphazard act of a mindless being or a trial and error result of some imagined evolution. It was the loving and purposeful act of our Creator.

He is God; He knows what He is doing; and He has everything under control. He carefully planned everything that exists, and absolutely nothing happened by accident. Each of us is here by design, and each of us has a purpose in life.

When God created Adam and Eve in His own image, He had a purpose in mind for them. He laid out that purpose clearly in Genesis 1:28:

And God said, Let us make man in our image, after our likeness: and let them have dominion over the fish of the sea, and over the fowl of the air, and over the cattle, and over all the earth, and over every creeping thing that creepeth upon the earth. So God created man in his own image, in the image of God created he him; male and female created he them. And God blessed them, and God said unto them, Be fruitful, and multiply, and replenish the earth, and subdue it: and have dominion over the fish of the sea, and over the fowl of the air, and over every living thing that moveth upon the earth.

Genesis 1:26-28

God's Purpose for the Individual

It is sad these days to see so many people stumbling aimlessly through life, wondering what their place is in the overall scheme of things, wondering if they have any real reason for living, wondering if their birth was an accident of nature. I want to shout out to them:

GOD DIDN'T MAKE A MISTAKE WITH YOU!

The sacred Scriptures teach us clearly that we are all here by design. We are predestined or *"predestinated,"* as the Apostle Paul says here, in his letter to the Ephesian believers.

You are not an accident of nature. You are not an aimless wanderer on the Earth. You were not born to stumble through life having no goal, no rudder to guide you, and no ultimate destination. God planned you before He made the Earth for you to live on. He planned you before He created plant and animal life for you to eat. He planned you before He placed the stars and the planets in their course. You are predestined of God, *"according to the purpose of Him who worketh all things after the counsel of His own will."* And God doesn't make any mistakes.

God had a purpose for the twin sons of Isaac and Rebekah, Jacob and Esau:

(For the children being not yet born, neither having done any good or evil, that the purpose of God according to election might stand, not of works, but of him that calleth.) Romans 9:11

It didn't matter that one of these sons loved God and the other didn't. God knew that fact from the beginning. Yet, He gave both of these boys life and the opportunity to choose the pathway each would take in life. What a loving God we serve!

God even had a purpose for the evil Pharaoh of Egypt:

For the scripture saith unto Pharaoh, Even for this same purpose have I raised thee up, that I might shew my power in thee, and that my name might be declared throughout all the earth.

Romans 9:17

Since God foresaw that the Pharaoh would reject Him, He used the Egyptian leader for the purpose of showing forth His mighty power in the days of Moses. Every time Pharaoh tried to stop God's people from going forth from Egypt in liberty, God manifested His mighty power in some other form. So God was glorified in the Pharaoh's rebellion.

God's Purpose for the Individual

God has a divine purpose for everything and for everybody. He even has a divine purpose for Satan. The devil had his chance to serve God, as Lucifer, the exalted angel, but he "blew it." God knew from the beginning of time that Lucifer would rebel and fall from heaven; yet he allowed him to exist anyway. His divine purpose in doing so was to present an alternative to men and women, to see if they really loved their Creator.

Everything has a purpose. The Scriptures declare it to be true:

To every thing there is a season, and a time to every purpose under the heaven: a time to be born, and a time to die; a time to plant, and a time to pluck up that which is planted; a time to kill, and a time to heal; a time to break down, and a time to build up; a time to weep, and a time to laugh; a time to mourn, and a time to dance; a time to cast away stones, and a time to gather stones together; a time to embrace, and a time to refrain from embracing; a time to get, and a time to lose; a time to keep, and a time to cast away; a time to rend, and a time to sew; a time to keep silence, and a time to speak; a time to love, and a time to hate; a time of war, and a time of peace. Ecclesiastes 3:1-8

Everything has a purpose, and every person has a purpose. You are important to God. He planned you. He created you. You are not an accident of nature. God has a purpose for you, and that purpose is *"eternal."*

> *According to the eternal purpose which he purposed in Christ Jesus our Lord.*
> Ephesians 3:11

You are not destined to failure; you are destined to greatness. You are not destined to poverty; you are destined to riches. You are not destined to sickness and death; you are destined to life and health.

We can easily see, however, that sometimes the good that God has ordained for a man or a woman is never realized. In the case of Lucifer, for instance, God created him as a glorious angel, not a wicked devil. The Scriptures describe him before his fall as *"son of the morning"* (Isaiah 14:12). He was said to be *"full of wisdom, and perfect in beauty"* (Ezekiel 28:12). God didn't make a mistake with Lucifer.

> *Thou wast perfect in thy ways from the day that thou wast created, till iniquity was found in thee.*
> Ezekiel 28:15

God's Purpose for the Individual

Lucifer lost this lofty estate because he *"sinned"* against God (Verse 16). His beauty caused him to become proud and think that he no longer needed his Creator. So he rebelled against God and fell, only to become the evil being we all know too well. God created him *"perfect,"* but he chose another path in life.

Jacob and Esau, likewise, had to choose a path to take in life. Jacob chose to respect and honor his Creator, and he prospered. Esau, on the other hand, chose to despise his spiritual heritage and to seek, instead, anything and everything that life could offer him, believing that real life was to be found in momentary pleasures. God called him a *"profane person"* (Hebrews 12:16) and pronounced him cursed (see Malachi 1:3-4).

The lesson is clear: those who respect God's purpose and live for Him prosper in life, while those who do not will have a very sad end.

This same story can be found over and over in the Bible and over and over in daily life. We cannot expect to prosper when we reject God's purpose for our existence.

And what is that purpose? When God created man, His purpose was expressed:

And God said, Let us make man in our image, after our likeness: and let them have dominion over the fish of the sea, and over the fowl of the air, and over the cattle, and over all the earth, and over every creeping thing that creepeth upon the earth. Genesis 1:26

God created man like Himself. He had already created a great variety of plant and animal life. If He had only wanted a private zoo, it was more than complete, but God longed for something else from His creation.

The second hint we get of God's purpose for man is that God came down and walked and talked with Adam and Eve in the Garden where He placed them. This shows us clearly that God's purpose for man is to have fellowship with Him.

We could say, then, that apart from knowing God and having fellowship with Him, life has little meaning for men and cannot be satisfying or ultimately rewarding.

But Adam and Eve, like Lucifer, chose not to obey God and fell from their exalted position in the Garden. It was then that man entered into a period of hopelessness and despair, of passing through life without knowing his reason for liv-

God's Purpose for the Individual

ing, without having someone to guide him into the true benefits of life and without having hope of eternal reward.

When Jesus came into the world, He called men to return to God, by faith, and to restore their relationship with the Creator, to be saved and return to God's purpose for their lives:

> *Who hath saved us, and called us with an holy calling, not according to our works, but according to his own purpose and grace, which was given us in Christ Jesus before the world began.*
> 2 Timothy 1:9

It is through faith in Jesus Christ and through establishing a personal relationship with Him that each individual can find God and find a purpose for living, a holy calling to a divine and eternal destiny. And it is upon this relationship that all other relationships must be based.

If we cannot properly relate to God and His purpose for our lives, nothing will go well for us in life. Our marriage cannot possibly be blessed. Our family cannot possibly prosper. We cannot hope to have God's favor upon us in this life, much less hope for a life to come.

Building a strong relationship with the Lord Jesus Christ is the vital first step to finding God's order for your family. →

Chapter 2

God's Purpose for Marriage and the Family

And the LORD God said, It is not good that the man should be alone; I will make him an help meet for him.

And the LORD God caused a deep sleep to fall upon Adam, and he slept: and he took one of his ribs, and closed up the flesh instead thereof; And the rib, which the LORD God had taken from man, made he a woman, and brought her unto the man. And Adam said, This is now bone of my bones, and flesh of my flesh: she shall be called woman, because she was taken out of man. Therefore shall a man leave his father and his mother, and shall cleave unto his wife: and they shall be one flesh.

Genesis 2:18 and 21-24

Marriage was ordained by God. It was His idea. Eve was God's gift to Adam, and Adam was God's gift to Eve. Eve was given to Adam to make him complete. He was incomplete without her. And Adam was given to Eve to make her complete. She was incomplete without him.

Marriage was not intended by God to be a battlefield. It was not intended to be a contest of wills or of who can shout the loudest. Marriage was ordained by God for a divine and eternal purpose and was meant, by God, to be a foretaste of Heaven.

In scripture, marriage is compared to our eventual union with God in eternity and should be, therefore, the nearest thing to Heaven we can experience here on this Earth:

> *For this cause shall a man leave his father and mother, and shall be joined unto his wife, and they two shall be one flesh. This is a great mystery: but I speak concerning Christ and the church.*
> Ephesians 5:31-32

So marriage is ordained of God and founded in His love. He desires to place His live in our hearts and allow us to express love to each other. God is love:

> *He that loveth not knoweth not God; for God is love.* 1 John 4:8

God's Purpose for Marriage and the Family

God is love; and he that dwelleth in love dwelleth in God, and God in him.   1 John 4:16

God's creation is an expression of His love, and marriage is not only the expression of love between a man and a woman, it is the expression of God's love. Marriage, then, should be blessed of God. But when we leave God out of our personal lives and out of our marriage, the purpose of God is defeated and marriage becomes something other than what God intended it to be. It becomes a battlefield of two contending personalities. What was meant to be heavenly becomes a Hell on Earth.

Just as Lucifer turned into the enemy of God and of God's people, when you fail to give God His proper place in your life and to submit to His will for you and your marriage, you lose the blessings meant for marriage, and your marriage degenerates into something totally different.

Marriage, the mystical union, is not just a joining of the flesh. It is a miracle of the joining of two persons into a single unit, and it can only be done by God Himself. Leave God out of marriage, and marriage becomes meaningless or worse.

God's second purpose for marriage is procreation.

And God blessed them, and God said unto them, Be fruitful, and multiply, and replenish the earth, and subdue it: and have dominion over the fish of the sea, and over the fowl of the air, and over every living thing that moveth upon the earth.

Genesis 1:28

God has given us the privilege of experiencing the miracle of conception and birth, a miracle which brings into the world those souls whom God has ordained to life, as He has us. This is a responsibility which most of us are taking far too lightly, as if it just happens. The birth of a child, any child, doesn't just happen. It is a miracle of God with a divine and eternal purpose.

Just as you were not a mistake of nature, your children were also not mistakes of nature. Our failure as a society to recognize God's purpose for each human life has led to the modern-day tragedy of the abortion of millions of unborn children. Every new soul was conceived in the heart of God in the ageless past, receives the breath of God and is born into the mystery of life. What a privilege it is to be a parent!

But bringing children into this world is only the beginning. When God entrusts them into our care, He expects us to create for them the proper environment

God's Purpose for Marriage and the Family

in which they can best grow and thrive. That proper environment is a loving and caring atmosphere, a godly atmosphere, a wholesome atmosphere, a safe atmosphere; and creating and maintaining such an atmosphere is a huge responsibility.

It is time that we get serious about fulfilling our God-given responsibilities toward every member of the family.

Marriage and family were ordained by God for our good, for our happiness, for the benefit of our souls. When we leave God out of our plans, when we fail to obey His Word in regard to our responsibilities as husband or wife, father or mother, son or daughter, brother or sister, the result can only be heartache and pain. No wonder our world is in such a mess! We have gone too far from God. It is time to come back to Him and, with His help, begin finding and applying His order for the family.

God is expecting much of us, for He has entrusted much into our hands. It is up to each of us what we do with what He has placed in our hands.

What you are is God's gift to you, and what you become is your gift to God. Your marriage is God's gift to you. Your children are God's gifts to you. And you will answer to God for how you treat the souls entrusted to your care and what you make of them.

What your marriage becomes is your gift to God, what your home becomes is your gift to God, what your children become is your gift to God. Is it a worthy one? Some day you will stand before God and give an account of all that you have done with His gifts to you. Will that be a happy day?

God does not expect you to have a perfect marriage. He knows that the two of you are not perfect people. He also knows that there are many enemies of a good marriage and that every marriage has its hard times. But He *is* expecting you to turn to Him in your hard times and to get His answer to your problems.

God does not expect you to have a perfect family. He knows that it is made up of imperfect people. And He knows that there are many enemies of a good home. But He *does* expect you to turn to Him in your time of trouble and get His answer to your problems.

When we turn to God, we find that He does, indeed, have answers. He does understand what we are facing. He can give us wisdom. He is more than able to help us resolve our personal conflicts and to be the victorious family He has destined us to be.

Many of our problems stem from our rejection, as a society, of God's order for the family. God

God's Purpose for Marriage and the Family

knew what He was doing when He placed a man and a woman together and gave them a child or a group of children. His order is important. There is a divine role for each member of the family to play.

First, God has placed the man as priest of his family. He is to be the spiritual example, to set the tone, to hear from God for the family, to receive direction for the family and to communicate that direction to the other members of the family. We might liken his role to the legislative branch of the government. He sets the family on the correct path.

This is a great responsibility and demands seriousness and dedication of our men, a seriousness and dedication that many are unwilling to make. So, our first problem is that men don't want to be men.

Secondly, God gave Adam a helpmeet. He saw that Adam could not do the job alone. He was incomplete. God made him a partner. Her name was Eve. As Adam's partner, Eve could look at things from a different perspective and keep Adam on course. She had the "woman's touch."

She was not Adam, she was not the man, but that didn't make her any less important. She was an equal partner in the marriage and in the responsibilities of the home. We might liken her to the executive branch of the government. She carried out the direction Adam received from God.

When the marriage is properly constituted, the husband is the husband, and the wife is the wife. The father is the father, and the mother is the mother. This is an irreversible arrangement, and when you try to reverse it, you are only asking for trouble. The position of husband and wife are not interchangeable. The two cannot change places. The wife cannot assume the authority of the husband. And the husband cannot cede his position to the wife.

God knows what He is doing. He has formed a family, with a variety of personalities, with a variety of talents, with a variety of abilities, and the positions He has decreed for the various members cannot be altered. They cannot be turned around.

The problem sometimes is that the husband doesn't want to be the spiritual leader in the home and allows the wife to assume his responsibility. He wants her to do it. When he does that, the troubles begin, for he is departing from the pattern the Lord has set for his family.

Husband, you are the priest of your family. It is sad to see many wives who have to take on this role because the husband lacks spiritual stamina, lacks spiritual insight, lacks spiritual strength. And because

God's Purpose for Marriage and the Family

the wife is more spiritually inclined than the husband, this role falls to her by forfeit. The wife becomes the priest of the household, and the husband just tags along. Because of that, he loses his spiritual authority.

If the woman of the house has to do the work of the pastor, the proper order of the house is disrupted, and that household is headed for trouble. Authority in the house was meant to rest on spiritual insight. That must be the basis of the authority.

It is the responsibility of the husband to see to the spiritual welfare of the family. The only case in which the woman is automatically in charge in this area is when the husband is not saved. In that case, women, you must "take up the slack" and do what is necessary to reinforce the spiritual foundations of your household. If not, you and your children will resemble dried prunes spiritually, and the negative influence of your husband will carry the members of the family into a worldly current.

When both husband and wife are Christians, the husband must assume the responsibility of priest of the family. Those men who have not performed willingly and well this function will have to answer to God on the judgment day.

In certain cases, when husbands are away for long periods, such as the case of military people or those working abroad, the husband should delegate this responsibility to his wife in his absence. She will execute his orders in his absence.

Marriage, under the best of circumstances, is not an easy proposition. Single people have enough problems on their own. They have problems living with themselves. How much more when they begin living with a stranger! Sometimes we can't stand ourselves, much less someone new. We have difficulty understanding ourselves, why we do the things we do. How much more difficult it is to understand others!

Once we are married, we have to not only understand ourselves but to make ourselves understood by this stranger we have, for some reason, chosen to live with. For marriage to work at all, it has to be a miracle.

When you decided to marry that woman, when you decided to marry that man, you relinquished your total independence and many of your rights and privileges. Marriage is a whole new world. You are not that individual you once were. You are now part of a team, part of a new unit. If, as you go along in your new world, you keep insisting on bringing up your old world or of having its benefits, your marriage will never be successful.

God's Purpose for Marriage and the Family

You must bury the past. You gave that up already, so stop trying to bring it back. You are now living in a new and different world. Your new kingdom has two equal rulers, the king and the queen. You cannot live in selfishness any longer. You have someone else to consider — in every sense of the word.

Before anyone takes the plunge into marriage, he or she needs to understand the seriousness of this act of union and to make up their minds if they are willing or not to lay aside their own ways and to adapt to a totally new reality. Those who have already taken that step can never look back.

I was married only a few days when I discovered that I was no longer independent. I was answerable to someone, my wife. I could no longer just do what I wanted to do and go where I wanted to go. I was part of a unit, part of a team.

When I was single, I could just jump up and go anywhere I wanted at a moment's notice. I was never pressed to return home. I could spend the night somewhere else if I wanted to. I was never worried about the time. No one was waiting for me at home. I didn't have to be concerned that when I came home too late, I would find the door locked. But there are consequences to the agreement we call marriage and we need to consider them carefully and decide if we are willing or not to keep our part of the bargain. Later is too late.

Getting married is very similar to our entrance into the Kingdom of God. In order to experience God's new life, we must first experience death to self and the old life. We must die before we can begin to live. That is also true of marriage. We must be willing to lay aside completely the old life of independence in order to begin a new life of mutual submission. Jesus said:

> *If any man will come after me, let him deny himself, and take up his cross, and follow me.*
> Matthew 16:24

Most of us, instead of denying ourselves, start insisting on having our rights. A common refrain of our day is: "I know my rights. How can you expect me to give up my rights?" But when we come to Jesus and enter into His Kingdom, we give up all personal rights and think, instead, of His will for our lives.

When we enter into a marriage contract, we lose all liberties and independence and become totally accountable to our mates, our partners in life. Wives have forfeited their rights to their hus-

God's Purpose for Marriage and the Family

bands, and husbands have forfeited their rights to their wives.

Face it. You have no rights now. You belong to each other.

> *Let the husband render unto the wife due benevolence: and likewise also the wife unto the husband. The wife hath not power of her own body, but the husband: and likewise also the husband hath not power of his own body, but the wife. Defraud ye not one the other, except it be with consent for a time, that ye may give yourselves to fasting and prayer; and come together again, that Satan tempt you not for your incontinency.*
>
> 1 Corinthians 7:3-5

In the Church, Christ has all the rights; and, in the marriage, your partner has all the rights. You have forfeited your rights. Husband, you have no more rights of your own. You cannot just pick up and go anytime you decide to do it. Your time is not your own anymore. Your days belong to your wife.

Wife, your time is not your own any longer. It is now under the control of your husband. He holds your rights. You are living for him now, not for yourself.

Founded On the Rock

In marriage, the wife holds the husband's rights and the husband holds the wife's rights; and, in this way, you are submitted to each other in God.

You have no right to be offended. You have no right to complain. You have no right to always get exactly what you want. You gave up your rights when you said those fateful words, "I DO." So, there is nothing to argue about.

The same principle that applies to our relationship to Jesus Christ, applies to our marriage. The moment you said, *"I DO,"* you meant:

I DO give you all my rights.
I DO give you all that I am.
Through thick and thin, I am yours.
I DO!
I DO!
I DO!
And, whether you like it or not, you are mine, as well.

These are simple principles, but they are dynamite, and when you put them into operation, I guarantee that your way of thinking will change, your attitude will change, and your behavior will change. Your home will be revolutionized.

God's Purpose for Marriage and the Family

We are all very concerned about our personal reputations. Your reputation is what other people think about you, their evaluation of you, what the community has to say about you. When we get married, however, we lose all personal identity and we become, instead, identified as "the mate of _____."

This is easier to see in the case of the woman, who even has to take on a totally different name. Suddenly, her driver's license and social security card must be changed. She has a new identity. We should probably change the name of the man too. That would make us realize that everything has changed. That simple "I do" changes EVERYTHING.

Marriage is very much like making a cake. The cake is made up of very different ingredients. But when you blend everything together, you can no longer see the eggs. They disappeared in the whole. You can no longer trace the flour. It has lost its identity. Everything is mixed together, and a more wonderful thing has emerged, something entirely different. A cake is not flour, and it is not eggs. It is something new and wonderful.

Now, the individuality of the husband is lost, and the individuality of the wife is lost. When you look at the cake (the marriage), you cannot see the husband, and you cannot see the wife. They are blended together. They are no longer separate individuals. They are now "one flesh."

No trace of those individuals can be found. All that they previously were has taken on a new nature. They are one. What belongs to the husband belongs to the wife. They are one and the same.

This is a TOTAL change of lifestyle, and most of us are not prepared for these changes. Many couples, in fact, are totally unprepared for what lies ahead. In their emotion, they want to get married. Never mind, they think, that there is no money to support the family, no money for the baby to be born in the hospital. Maybe they can get food stamps and free milk from some public program. The couple that thinks like this has no business getting married. This may seem farfetched to some, but far too many of those who are tying the knot these days are totally unprepared, have no idea what marriage is and less idea of what is expected of them. No wonder we have so many modern-day tragedies!

This is the reason I highly recommend to anyone contemplating marriage to seek marriage counseling. As the traditional marriage ceremony declares:

God's Purpose for Marriage and the Family

It is not by any to be entered into unadvisedly or lightly; but reverently, discreetly, advisedly, soberly and in the fear of God.

I personally refuse to perform a marriage ceremony for any couple not wanting to take marriage counseling. Marriage is a serious business.

The first step in finding God's order for your family is to recognize His plan for the family and to become willing to follow His plan. In this regard, parents are not the only guilty parties. Children are children. They are immature. They have little wisdom. They are incapable of making mature decisions. They are, therefore, to be in subjection to their parents, not so that they lose all the fun of living, but for their own welfare.

When children begin to tell their parents what to do, to make immature demands and to get their way, when children begin to pilot the family ship, the whole process goes berserk and must end in a flaming crash. Yet, in the day in which we are living, many children begin to make their own decisions at a very early age, and it is considered detrimental to their mental health not to let them have their way in everything they want. How can we function as a society if children are making all the decisions? No wonder we are so far off course! It is time to begin finding God's order for your family. →

Chapter 3

The Importance of a Strong Foundation

To whom coming, as unto a living stone, disallowed indeed of men, but chosen of God, and precious, Ye also, as lively stones, are built up a spiritual house, an holy priesthood, to offer up spiritual sacrifices, acceptable to God by Jesus Christ. Wherefore also it is contained in the scripture, Behold, I lay in Sion a chief corner stone, elect, precious: and he that believeth on him shall not be confounded. Unto you therefore which believe he is precious: but unto them which be disobedient, the stone which the builders disallowed, the same is made the head of the corner.

1 Peter 2:4-7

The strength of every structure depends on the strength of the foundation upon which it is built. In the same way, every relationship, even a friendship, depends on the foundation upon which that relationship is built.

Your most important relationship is with God, and your relationship with Him will only be productive when your spiritual house is built upon a solid foundation. When that foundation is strong, you can be faithful to God through thick and thin, through every trial and turmoil.

A right relationship with God will bring you into a right relationship with your spouse and with your children. When you are spiritually cold, backslidden and indifferent, you become an unbearable husband, or you become a nagging wife. You become an insufferable parent, or you become a rebellious and disobedient son or daughter.

But when you are doing well in your relationship with God, nothing is too difficult for you to face in life. You stop looking at the negative aspects of life, the dark shadows that we all pass through from time to time, and you start looking at the positive side of things. The problems that you may face do not discourage you because you know that God can turn around any situation to His glory and honor. You know that He loves you and that He is working with your best interests at heart. Then, you can say, like the Apostle Paul:

The Importance of a Strong Foundation

And we know that all things work together for good to them that love God, to them who are the called according to his purpose. Romans 8:28

What a difference a good foundation makes! Get the foundation right, and everything else will follow. The Psalmist David knew the importance of proper foundations. He said:

If the foundations be destroyed, what can the righteous do? Psalm 11:3

Nothing could be more important than laying a proper foundation. And what is the proper foundation for a marriage and for a home? It is the same as the proper foundation for an individual or for a congregation. Our foundation, as Christians, is Jesus Himself. Paul said:

For other foundation can no man lay than that is laid, which is Jesus Christ. 1 Corinthians 3:11

Christ is the *"cornerstone"* of our building:

And are built upon the foundation of the apostles and prophets, Jesus Christ himself being the chief

corner stone; In whom all the building fitly framed together groweth unto an holy temple in the Lord:
Ephesians 2:20-21

The inspired hymn writer penned the words:

On Christ the Solid Rock I stand.
All other ground is sinking sand.

It is true. Get founded on the Rock Christ Jesus, and you will be surprised when the storms of life pass you by. Everything else around you will be falling, but you will stand. You cannot fall — when you are planted firmly on THE ROCK.

We are the *"lively stones"* the Lord uses to build a meaningful structure upon that precious foundation of Christ. Every member of the family — husband, wife, and children — must form part of that building, constructed upon that sure and firm foundation.

Jesus taught about the need for a solid foundation in His Sermon on the Mount:

Therefore whosoever heareth these sayings of mine, and doeth them, I will liken him unto a wise man, which built his house upon a rock: And the rain descended, and the floods came, and the winds

The Importance of a Strong Foundation

blew, and beat upon that house; and it fell not: for it was founded upon a rock. And every one that heareth these sayings of mine, and doeth them not, shall be likened unto a foolish man, which built his house upon the sand: And the rain descended, and the floods came, and the winds blew, and beat upon that house; and it fell: and great was the fall of it.   Matthew 7:24-27

This word *"therefore"* signifies a conclusion or a summary of the whole teaching at hand, and the summary or conclusion is always important. So these are important words. We should give heed to them.

There is another reason these words are so important. Jesus said *"Whosoever heareth these sayings of MINE."* These are not my words; these are the words of Jesus. What He says merits our full attention.

Hearing, however, is not enough. We have too many Christians who only hear and do not respond. Responding positively to what we hear is what produces results. *"Faith without works is dead."*

But wilt thou know, O vain man, that faith without works is dead?   James 2:20

Founded On the Rock

For as the body without the spirit is dead, so faith without works is dead also. James 2:26

Many marriages suffer from a lack of proper works. It is possible to say to your spouse, "Honey, I love you," or "Darling, you mean everything to me," but if you do the opposite of what you are saying, your lovely words will get you nowhere. Your wife is not stupid. Your husband is not dumb. He or she knows whether your love is genuine or only a pretense. And the Lord is not ignorant either. He knows the sincerity of our hearts. Let's get serious with God about the development of a proper home, with Jesus Christ as the foundation.

Why are relationships so important? Studies show that we spend ninety percent of our time relating to other people in some way: at work, in the marketplace, at home, at church. The relationships we form may be good, or they may be bad. Nothing does more to develop happiness and a sense of well-being than developing happy, healthy relationships with other people.

With some people we develop only a shallow or superficial relationship. With others, we may even be hypocritical and develop a relationship similar to that of the scribes and Pharisees. As Christians,

The Importance of a Strong Foundation

however, we are motivated, encouraged and admonished by God that our relationships, our outward manifestation of righteousness, must reach far beyond the righteousness of the scribes and the Pharisees:

> *For I say unto you, That except your righteousness shall exceed the righteousness of the scribes and Pharisees, ye shall in no case enter into the kingdom of heaven.* Matthew 5:20

The scribes and the Pharisees were hypocrites, pretenders, actors. You cannot build a proper relationship with this material. If you don't get beyond pretension, God rejects your righteousness. Learn to be genuine with God and man. Learn to be open and aboveboard with all your dealings. Nobody likes a phony. Build your house on THE ROCK.

The foolish man built his house upon the sand. He built a house, but he built it on mere emotion; he built it on mere excitement. Then, like so many others, he woke up one day on the wrong side of the bed and wasn't in the mood to be loving to his wife. His relationship was shallow; it was built upon soft ground; there was nothing solid in it. So it didn't last.

This man had based his relationship upon the

Founded On the Rock

weather. If the sun was shining, he was sunny too. If it was raining, however, he was grouchy. No wonder so many marriages fail! No wonder so many children run away from home! Nobody wants to live in that kind of atmosphere.

The foundation of your home, the foundation of your marriage and the foundation of your family, is very important, and the most important thing to do is to get Jesus involved in your life. Get Him involved in your marriage. Get Him involved in your family.

Jesus is the best Designer, the best Architect. He has given us a blueprint, with all the proper specifications necessary for building the temple of our lives and of our homes. We must build according to His plan.

Don't try to take shortcuts. If something is a little too long, cut it. Don't try to fit in something that is not matched to God's plan. If something is too short, extend it or join it to another piece or get a longer piece. Don't risk building a faulty house. If something is loose, tighten it. Every piece must fit together properly. We must prepare a temple, fit for the Master's use.

Don't try to do all the work yourself. You will only bungle the job. Jesus is the best Carpenter. Let Him

The Importance of a Strong Foundation

do the work in your life. He is the Master Builder. If you depend on Him, your home will be rock solid, and nothing will be able to harm you.

One of the most important parts of Jesus' teaching to remember is that the storms *will* come, the rain *will* descend, the floods *will* come, the winds *will* blow. Expect adversity in your life. It is not a bad thing and will not do you any harm — if you are properly prepared. God uses adversity to test us and to show us His power.

If you don't have the Lord present with you, then adversity is truly a tragedy. Those winds will blow your house down. Those floods will carry away all the things you count precious in life. Those rains will descend relentlessly upon you until little will remain of the life you have built together. *"Great was the fall of it."*

Storms will surely come, so don't try to face life without the Lord. Get your foundations properly secured, and you will have nothing to worry about. Let men say of your marriage and of your home, *"It fell not: for it was founded upon a rock."*

Let us now begin to lay that proper foundation that will insure us victory over life's adversities. Don't skip over a single step, for each one is important. Get each piece in place, and all solidly interlocked.

And soon you will be singing the praises of the God who gives you victory.

Don't delay. Begin finding God's order for your family. →

Part II

Building a Strong Foundation for Your Home

Chapter 4

The Foundation of Agreement

Again I say unto you, That if two of you shall agree on earth as touching any thing that they shall ask, it shall be done for them of my Father which is in heaven. Matthew 18:19

Can two walk together, except they be agreed?
Amos 3:3

In a successful marriage there must be agreement. In any relationship, this can prove difficult. Because we are different individuals, because we come from different backgrounds and think in different ways, it is not easy to agree on anything, let alone on everything. In this area, we Christians have a wonderful advantage.

When we come to the Lord Jesus Christ, we surrender our will to Him and agree with Him. Making

Him Lord and Savior of our lives requires that we come to absolute surrender to Him and absolute reliance upon Him. We give up our identities, our own natures, to comprehend, accept, and join with His divine nature. We lose our own identities as we step out of ourselves into an intimate relationship with the Lord Jesus Christ.

> *Whereby are given unto us exceeding great and precious promises: that by these ye might be partakers of the divine nature, having escaped the corruption that is in the world through lust.*
> 2 Peter 1:4

As we take on the nature of Christ, all of our sinfulness is covered by His righteousness. All of our Adamic nature is covered by His own pure nature. In reality, we no longer live, but Christ lives in us.

> *I am crucified with Christ: nevertheless I live; yet not I, but Christ liveth in me: and the life which I now live in the flesh I live by the faith of the Son of God, who loved me, and gave himself for me.*
> Galatians 2:20

The Foundation of Agreement

When Christ lives in us, we begin to live to glorify God the Father in the members of our body. And, in that way, we come to total agreement with Him, by yielding to His perfect will for us. In a very real sense, we give up our own mind and take on the mind of Christ. As Paul taught:

But we have the mind of Christ.
1 Corinthians 2:16
Let this mind be in you, which was also in Christ Jesus:
Philippians 2:5

Not every believer learns this secret or is willing to submit himself to the will of God, and, because of that, we often have disagreements in the church. It is not uncommon to have some members leave because of some insignificant point of disagreement.

One common point of disagreement in the church is that someone doesn't like the color of the carpet. In one of the churches I pastored, I experienced a similar problem. We moved the piano, and some of the members did not like the new location. "For twenty years," they said, "that piano has been in the same spot. Why does it need to be moved?" And they left the church — because the piano had been moved.

That illustrates the problem of agreement. God wanted to take the monotony out of the lives of those believers and to give them some beautiful, new, and exciting things, but they couldn't agree on it.

That is exactly the problem we are confronting in the home. Husbands and wives cannot agree, and their disagreement brings them great heartache. God wants to join us together, not just physically, but in our desires. And the only way we can do that is if we both agree with the Lord and let Him rule our lives. We may not agree on every point of taste and style, but we should be able to agree in our spirits because we both love the Lord and want His will for our lives.

If the husband says, "I am going this way," and the wife says, "Go ahead, but I am going this other way," that doesn't make for a very happy marriage. The children will say, "If you are each going your own way, we will just go our own way too," and they will go off in yet another direction. When this happens, the family degenerates into a constant tug of war.

As very different individuals, we cannot expect to have all the same tastes and likes and dislikes in life. We can, however, agree to submit together to the will of God for our lives. We can be willing to be

The Foundation of Agreement

joined together in purpose and intent. This will put us on the same course in life. At least we will all be headed in the same direction. If we have one destiny, one vision, and one desire, and that one desire is to glorify the name of Jesus, we can work out our other differences. Anything that doesn't lend itself to this unity of purpose must be put under subjection to the mind of Christ.

This type of agreement can only work if God is in the picture. No matter how much two people might agree with each other, if they do not get into agreement with God, nothing good can come of it.

Agreement is powerful. Paul and Silas, two very different individuals, were in agreement in the Philippian jail.

> *And at midnight Paul and Silas prayed, and sang praises unto God: and the prisoners heard them. And suddenly there was a great earthquake, so that the foundations of the prison were shaken: and immediately all the doors were opened, and every one's bands were loosed.* Acts 16:25-26

As these two men prayed together and sang together, their agreement rocked the jail and set them free. There is power and strength in agreement. We all need more of it — in all our relationships. And this type of agreement is reached only when each of us frees himself from all preconceived ideas and fully submits to the Lordship of Jesus Christ.

The husband cannot approach the marriage with the old-fashioned idea that he is the head, regardless of whether he is right or wrong, and start bossing his wife around and treating her like his slave. Too many have done this. "Wife," they have declared, "From now on you are subject to me. You must obey me. Sit down! Stand up! Go get me a cup of coffee! Bring me my slippers! Where is the newspaper?"

This is a concept of headship adulterated by the thinking of the world. This is not a Christian concept. Yes, the husband is the head of the house, but the wife is the neck that turns the head. If you want to convince a man to do something, speak first with his wife. She has the power to convince him to do it. We are equal partners in marriage.

Husbands, get rid of your machismo and let God bless your home. Yes, you are the head, but you must govern your home in love. You must govern in grace. You must govern in understanding, in caring and in sharing. God did not set you up as a dictator in your home. God did not appoint you to be a tyrant over your loved ones. He has called you to hear His

The Foundation of Agreement

voice and to carry out His divine and eternal plan for those whom He has placed in your care.

Marriage is an equal partnership. In an equal partnership, no one is higher and no one is lower than another. We are all on the same level. There is a balance of power.

In the eyes of God, there are no males, and there are no females; there are no bond, and there are no free; there are no Jews, no Greeks, no barbarians. We are all children of God, equal in His sight.

> *There is neither Jew nor Greek, there is neither bond nor free, there is neither male nor female: for ye are all one in Christ Jesus.* Galatians 3:28

Husband, your wife is a child of God. Treat her with care. Wife, your husband is a child of the Lord. Treat him with care.

Husband, your wife is God's special gift to you. Be careful how you handle God's gift. Wife, your husband is God's special gift to you. Be careful how you handle God's special gift. Parents, your children are God's gift to you. Be careful how you handle that gift. Children, God has given you your parents as a special gift. Be careful how you treat them.

Husbands, you can say, "I am God's gift to my wife." Wives, you can say, "I am God's gift to my husband." And, listen to me well, both of you: God doesn't give any bad gifts. His gifts are all *"good and perfect."*

> *Every good gift and every perfect gift is from above, and cometh down from the Father of lights, with whom is no variableness, neither shadow of turning.* James 1:17

Don't despise God's gifts. Husbands, say to yourself. "My wife is the most beautiful woman in the world." Say it, and mean it. Wives, say this: "My husband is the best looking man in the world." How can I expect you to say that? You can say it with assurance because he is a gift from God to you, and God doesn't give us rotten eggs. God doesn't give us rotten tomatoes. He always gives us something that will be satisfying and exciting, something that will make us happy, fulfilled, and whole.

Agreement means covenant. A covenant is a legal document signed by two parties. In marriage we have covenanted to spend our lives together, not just the moments of ecstasy and physical enjoyment, but all times.

The Foundation of Agreement

There are some humdrum moments in life. There are times when it seems like we are spinning our wheels. We must cross through some dark places together. Life puts us through the wringer. There will be moments of financial instability. We will go around some dangerous curves together. There are a lot of twists and turns in life. But if the document is solid, and the two parties are in agreement, nothing can hinder our relationship.

Our contract is irrevocable before God. Stop wasting your time arguing over the petty thing that don't really matter at all. Twenty years from now, who will care what color the carpet was? When history records your life, who will care about those insignificant details? Stop allowing those things to hinder your relationship with the loved ones God has given you. Get into agreement, and, I promise you, God will begin to defeat all your enemies and to give you victory on every side.

Place your will in subjection to the will of God and take the first steps necessary to finding God's order for your family. ➜

Chapter 5

The Foundation of Unity

In those days there was no king in Israel, but every man did that which was right in his own eyes.
                                                                Judges 17:6

Agreement makes possible a certain unity in the family, but it does not happen automatically. We must work at it. Unity comes about through order. If everyone is doing his own thing, there can be no unity.

Families are divided because there is no strong leadership to unite them. Someone must impose order upon the household. Someone must know God's will for the entire family and impose upon it an organizational structure in keeping with that revelation. The family, like any other organization which is made up of several members, needs a program. The family, like any other organization, needs a schedule. Someone must produce that schedule, and God has entrusted that responsibility to parents.

The Foundation of Unity

When we are all going in different directions, each doing his or her own thing, the children are the most severely affected. They are bounced around with no clear idea of where they are going in life. They feel disoriented, as if they are floating about in the air.

No wonder so many of our Christian young people are lost! No wonder so many of them are running away from home! They don't know or understand what is going on in their homes. They live in the same house with the other members of the family, yet they have no idea what the organizational structure of the home is or if such a structure even exists. They have no idea what their bounds and limits are. Psychologists have shown that this causes insecurity and unhappiness in children and causes them to rebel against their parents.

Does it matter if our teenagers come home at two o'clock in the morning? Are parents bothered if their children are not in bed by midnight? Many parents don't seem to care. If their teenagers get drunk, they shrug their shoulders and say, "Well, he is not the only one. Everyone is doing it these days." And they think that pat answer excuses them from responsibility. But they are wrong. Nothing excuses us from executing our God-given responsibility to govern well our own households.

Proper government pays off. When the family is a unit, and every member of the family is a functioning part of that unit, everything changes. You have produced a winning team. When every member is given equal importance, and every member knows his place in the family, you can accomplish great things together. This takes a lot of wisdom on our part.

Parents must have wisdom from God to govern well their household. They are responsible to do the following:

- Establish schedules and programs for the entire family
- Establish accepted norms of conduct and make those norms of conduct known and understood by every member of the family
- Apply the proper discipline when these established norms of conduct are violated
- Give direction to every member of the family
- Train every family member in his or her respective duties
- Motivate every member of the family toward proper goals

The Foundation of Agreement

Even adult married people are often lacking in all of these areas. Therefore, the administration of our duties and responsibilities before God requires that we first bring ourselves under His control, that we hear His voice concerning our own lives, and that we obey His will and His Word for us as individuals.

Most parents fail to be proper parents because they are not proper individuals first. If we are not disciplined ourselves, what can we expect of our children? If we are not motivated ourselves, what can we expect of our children? If we have no certain goals in life or no certain norms of conduct, what can we expect of our children?

And when should we implement this special training of our children? At the earliest possible moment. Swimming instructors are now beginning to work with children at a very tender age. Through new studies we are learning that newborn infants have amazing senses. They can learn a lot, and they can learn it fast.

So, don't wait. Begin teaching your children at a very early age. They are not ignorant. They are not oblivious to what goes on around them. They are watching and listening and learning from the very first day. If you wait, you will miss many wonderful opportunities. Start teaching early — before your child becomes stubborn or spoiled.

Proper discipline is one of the most important elements of our training, and it is so misunderstood these days that I want to lay a firm groundwork for it here.

It is one thing to have recognized standards of conduct for the home and even to be sure that everyone understands those standards, but it is quite another thing to reinforce those standards, to apply consistent and fair discipline. God does it with us.

> *For whom the Lord loveth he chasteneth, and scourgeth every son whom he receiveth.*
> Hebrews 12:6

> *As many as I love, I rebuke and chasten: be zealous therefore, and repent.* Revelation 3:19

God says that He chastens us because He loves us. It would be unloving of Him not to do it. His great love compels Him to correct us when we go astray or disobey Him. He knows that our welfare depends on our keeping His statutes. They are not made for the purpose of robbing us of the joys of living. They are made to protect us from the tyranny of the dev-

The Foundation of Unity

il and from the fickleness of our own hearts. God knows what is best for us, and, because of that, He disciplines us when we do not obey Him. He does it because He loves us.

Young people should be thankful for strict parents. The fact that they are strict shows that they care. They love you or they wouldn't bother. It would be easier not to impose any guidelines for the family and not to ever punish anyone for any reason, but that would not be loving. Parents who love their children discipline them, just as God disciplines us because of His love.

When your children say, "If Susie can do that, why can't I?" just answer, "I can't answer for Susie's parents. I am your parent, and I feel that we cannot permit that." That is enough. You don't have to apologize for loving your children and wanting the best for them. The Bible is very clear on this point.

> *He that spareth his rod hateth his son: but he that loveth him chasteneth him betimes.*
> Proverbs 13:24

> *Chasten thy son while there is hope, and let not thy soul spare for his crying.* Proverbs 19:18

Foolishness is bound in the heart of a child; but the rod of correction shall drive it far from him.
Proverbs 22:15

Withhold not correction from the child: for if thou beatest him with the rod, he shall not die. Thou shalt beat him with the rod, and shalt deliver his soul from hell. Proverbs 23:13-14

The rod and reproof give wisdom: but a child left to himself bringeth his mother to shame.
Proverbs 29:15

Discipline is positive reinforcement, a teaching technique proven through many generations. Children won't soon forget properly administered discipline. "Properly administered" is the key phrase here. Just as God chastens us because He loves us, He always does it in a loving way.

Discipline cannot be done in anger. If it is done in anger, it has a negative effect, not a positive effect. When you are angry, cool off before you discipline your child, or you may be guilty of child abuse. Don't do anything when you are trembling with rage. Discipline only in love, never in anger.

If you try to talk to your wife about some differ-

The Foundation of Unity

ence you have when you are trembling with rage, you will end up hitting her and doing and saying other things for which you will later be sorry. Wait until you cool down to talk over your disagreement. You owe it to yourself, as well as to your wife and children.

Many people treat their children like animals, pulling their hair and slapping them hard across the face. That is not discipline, that is child abuse. Don't be guilty of such action.

When you spank your child, always let him know why you are doing it. Never spank him without giving an explanation. If you insist on spanking a child without telling him why, he learns nothing from it and only resents you and resents what you have done.

I remember being spanked by my mother and wondering why. I may well have done plenty of bad things, but she did not explain to me what I had done wrong and why I was being spanked. Sometimes she pinched me and broke the skin, and I had no idea why she was doing it, so I considered it to be cruel and determined to run away at the first opportunity. I was sure that she didn't love me.

Spanking can become an emotional outlet for parents' frustrations. That kind of spanking never produces the desired effect. That is not discipline, so avoid it.

The word *discipline* comes from the word *disciple* and means to teach something by reinforcing good behavior and punishing bad behavior. The kind of spankings and pinchings I am talking about teaches nothing, and it accomplishes nothing. It only breeds resentment. That is why the Bible says:

> *And, ye fathers, provoke not your children to wrath: but bring them up in the nurture and admonition of the Lord.* Ephesians 6:4

Don't be guilty of actions that only provoke your children and accomplish nothing positive. Tell your child what he has done wrong and exactly why you are giving him a spanking, or your efforts will be wasted.

Spanking is never easy for a parent who loves his child. It hurts you more than it hurts them. Beating a child, on the other hand, seems to be easy for a parent full of hatred and bitterness. But that is not discipline, and nothing good is accomplished.

Don't spank a child without first giving him a warning. Say *no* when a child reaches for the fire. Then, explain to that child why you are saying no.

The Foundation of Unity

Let him know that it is for his own good. You might say, "If you put your hand in there, you will get burned." If he keeps doing it, you may be forced to smack that hand for its own good, to maintain it whole.

Don't spank a child just anywhere on his body. Children can be very fragile. Use the spot God has reserved for spanking, the rump. It is well padded and can take your smacks without causing some permanent damage.

Then, when you have spanked a child, do not remain angry with him. Once you have done what you have to do, it is over. Now, take him in your arms and love him. Show him that you don't reject him for what he did. Say that you are sorry you had to do it but that it was for his own good.

This kind of discipline teaches the importance of respect and obedience and of following instructions. You will accomplish much good in this way. Discipline is not vengeance. It is a teaching method and a very proven teaching method at that.

Some parents decline to discipline their children when they are small, saying, "But she is just a little girl. She can't help herself." Then, when that child is grown, it is too late; she is already out of control. When this is the case, you haven't done her any favors by not exercising discipline. Your decision was not in her long-term interest. Sweet little boys and girls have a way of becoming holy terrors when they are not properly disciplined. Do what has to be done.

As your children get older, you must know where they are at all times. That is your responsibility. Never let them go out if where they are going or what they are going to do is unclear. Know exactly where they are going, know what time they are due home, and be sure they get home on time. If you never give any instructions, you cannot make any corrections. This is the cause of many problems in the house.

Father and mother, put yourselves in agreement concerning the discipline of the children. Don't allow the children to play one parent off against another. There must be agreement in discipline. If Mama said "NO," don't entertain the plea to change that decision. Mama, if your husband has said "NO," don't try to reverse that decision. Be supportive of each other. Speak with one voice.

When your child pleads with you, say, "I am sorry, your father has said 'NO,' so 'no' it is." That is why it is always better to talk these things over between the two of you and come to an agreement. You may not know all the details. Get the facts, then make a decision. If your child is asking to do some-

The Foundation of Unity

thing, tell him, "Give me time to talk this over with your father," or "Give me a moment to talk this over with your mother, then I will give you an answer." Make these decisions together.

Make household rules, and be sure your children know what you expect of them. If you don't, you have no right to complain later when they don't do what you expected. If you didn't tell them when to come home, you can't complain — no matter what time they come home.

If you told your teenager to be in before 11:00, and he came in at 12:15, you have every right to raise your voice and let him know that he cannot do that again. But if you didn't tell him to be in by 11:00, you cannot say anything. He is innocent.

Teenagers will go as far as you allow them to go. They will take every advantage you give them. They will do everything you allow them to do. They are depending on you for guidance, so don't fail them.

Be honest with yourself, and be honest with your mate, and God will help you make the proper decisions.

I certainly didn't know these things before I became a father. I learned by relating to my own children. I learned by crying out to God. Parenting is very challenging. It is both thrilling and exciting to accept that challenge and to watch God work in our lives. The joy of molding a young life is far beyond anything else we can experience.

Learning to deal properly with your children brings you closer together as a couple. You learn as much as the children learn. Then, when those children grow up and marry for themselves, they will not forget the lessons you have taught them. They will say to their children, "My mother always did it like this," or "My Daddy always did this to me, that's why I am doing it to you."

Dad, how many times have you taken your son for a walk and had a heart-to-heart talk with him? You can go fishing or go for a ride. Mom, how much time have you spent with your teenage daughter, having a heart-to-heart talk? Have you prepared her well to be a woman? Too many children are learning about sex in the wrong way and from the wrong people. You might say: "So, you have a boyfriend/a girlfriend now? Well, there are some things that you need to learn, and I want to teach you."

One of the suitors of my eldest daughter told the classmates of their school, "Watch out for Joy, because her mother is a real witch."

My wife was so protective of Joy that she would not allow her to go anywhere alone with a boy, even

The Foundation of Unity

if it was to a Christian gathering. "If you want to see our daughter," she told Joy's friend, "come to our house and see her." She would go into another room while the boy was there, but she felt more secure having them in our own house. Very few boys accepted her invitation.

Of course, that upset Joy. So, I talked to her and said: "Listen, Joy, I know it is hard, but it is for your own good." Once she understood the reasoning behind it and that she wasn't being deprived of life, she accepted it, and she didn't complain again.

We have to explain to our children why we do the things we do.

Many parents are not even aware that their children have an outside interest, a boyfriend or a girlfriend, because they are not close enough to them, and their children never tell them anything. If you work through the years on establishing a good relationship, and you become your children's best friend, they will tell you everything that is happening to them. Our children must not be afraid to come and tell us everything that is in their hearts. If we are close to them, they will talk to us before they talk to anyone else.

If you are aloof with your children, they will be aloof with you and afraid to come to you and open their hearts. They could be in trouble and you wouldn't even know it. You might be the last to know anything that is happening with your children.

If you have a good relationship with your children, they won't be able to hide things from you; and, furthermore, they won't want to hide things from you.

Parents have to ask many questions of their children to find out how everything is going in their schooling, etc., but if you are their friend, you won't even have to ask them about problems they are having. They will come to you and volunteer the information. Children love to confide in someone. If they cannot confide in you, they will find someone else in whom they may confide.

You are Mom or Dad, but you are also best friend. Many teenagers who are classified as "troubled" are that way because they have never been able to confide in their parents.

If you are just starting your family, you are learning this secret just in time. Make every effort to bring that family into such close unity that every member will be important to every other member, that every member will be given equal time and equal attention.

The Foundation of Unity

A well-known news program here in the United States, a few years ago, featured the case of a man and his son who abused more than five hundred children and took pornographic pictures of them, which they circulated for great profit. The main focus of the program was on how so many children could be abused and not report it. The answer was that they were afraid to tell. I guarantee that if they had grown up experiencing a good relationship with their parents, those children would have complained when those advances began, let alone after the evil deeds were already committed.

We must protect our children by living so closely to them that we know everything they are thinking and doing — always. If the home is a haven and a refuge where children feel loved and protected, cared for and respected, whenever they sense danger they are going to run to the arms of their parents. When you love children, they know it.

We think it is normal for children to hide many things from their parents, but that is not true. It is not normal. Children want to talk about their problems. They want to talk about their fears. It is hard for a child to keep a secret. They almost can't do it. They have the emotional need of talking about it with someone.

Never be too busy for your child. Never push him aside in impatience. Nothing is more important than your son. Nobody is more important than your daughter. This is something that we simply cannot afford to take for granted. This is IMPORTANT. And, if our problem is a matter of culture, we simply must change. We are living in the computer age, not the dark ages.

Your relationship to each other, as husband and wife, is directly affected by the success or failure of your relationship with your children. Do a good job raising your children, and your marriage will be strengthened. Fail, and you will pay for the rest of your life.

The very best way you can teach them is by your example. Live what you preach, and never expect anything of your children that you are not willing to do yourself.

If you quarrel with your spouse, do not do so in the hearing of your children. If you must do it, go into your room and close the door. Nothing is more devastating to children, nothing does more to destroy their sense of well-being, and nothing goes further to rob them of security than to hear their parents arguing. Make it a cardinal rule never to let it happen.

The Foundation of Unity

If you are having some misunderstanding, don't even let your children know about it. Even worse is to use your children as a tool to reach out to each other:

"Tell you dad it's time to eat."

"Dad, Mom said to tell you it's time to eat."

"Tell you mother that I can eat later. I don't want to eat at the same table with her."

When we are guilty of this sin, the children become pawns in our game. They actually become the chopping board where we try to cut each other to pieces. They are the backboard off of which we bounce each other.

When we do this, we put the children into a very difficult position. They feel compelled to take sides, but they don't know which side to take. They love both parents. They are emotionally torn. And, in the end, they will get angry with both father and mother and will resent the fact that their parents put them in this position.

In the middle of a fight, some parents start yelling at the children. "Who are you going with? Are you going with your dad? Oh, go ahead. Are you going with me? Come on then." The poor children are pulled in two. It happens all the time. This is the direct result of having a poor relationship.

Founded On the Rock

That is why it is so important to have a deep commitment, a solid understanding in your relationship and know where you stand with each other, as husband and wife. Come to an agreement on how to train your children, and keep that agreement.

As our children grow up into teenagers and are able to do much more work, it is good to give them certain responsibilities. We must not allow them to be lazy. We must not, also, give our children more than they can handle. Don't overwork them. They have very small shoulders. Do not give them responsibilities beyond their ability, and do not relinquish your own responsibilities to them.

You might decide: "Tomorrow, at breakfast, I will wash the dishes. Since everyone is out at lunch time there will be nothing to wash. When we eat at dinner time, _____ (the oldest) will wash tonight. Then _____ (the second child) will wash tomorrow night and _____ (the third child) will take a turn the next night." Children can help clean the house, take out the trash, make the beds, and many other similar tasks.

As your children grow up, they must be incorporated into the activities of the household, or they will think they are not important, not needed. Have a division of labor, slowly developing and increasing

The Foundation of Unity

the responsibility until your children can be serious workers, capable of tackling anything in life.

The youngest child in the family may be the greatest challenge, for several reasons:

The oldest and youngest children in the family always receive more attention than the others: the oldest, because there were no other siblings yet to compete for attention in the home, and the youngest, because of being the last to leave home. The oldest child learns responsibility and the exercise of authority through caring for the younger ones. The oldest is very accustomed to hearing: "Do this!" and "Do that!"

But, by the time the youngest is old enough to take responsibility, there are no children left to care for. Younger children, therefore, often are spoiled and do not learn how to take responsibility and how to handle authority.

If you have built up a proper relationship, when you are separated from your children because of their studies or some other reason, you won't have to worry about them. And you will know that they will carry this healthy relationship into their own home, as well, after they get married.

As your children get more mature, you don't have to be nearly as rigid with them. Allow for a little give and take. Listen to their viewpoint and take it into account when making your decisions. If you want to be understood by them, be understanding. If you want to be loved by them, sow love into their lives. You always reap what you sow.

At what point do you break off the discipline? When my son was sixteen years old, I told him that I was still bigger than he was and that I could still take him on. Children are never too old for discipline. At that age, however, spankings are not very effective. You have to use more reasoning and other types of punishment. Taking away something your young person values seems to be effective for teenagers, for instance: grounding them for a certain period of time.

As long as your child is living under your roof, you are responsible before God for him. Tell him, "As long as you are eating at my table and sleeping in my house, I expect you to keep the rules of this house." It doesn't matter if he is forty years old. If he lives with you, he must submit to the rules you lay down.

Even if he is married, if he is still living under your roof (as is the case in many of our developing countries where employment is scarce), do not allow him to arbitrarily disregard your standards of

The Foundation of Unity

household conduct. Let him know what you expect of him, and make him uphold your standard. It is for the good of the entire household.

Until the day he moves to his own place, he is under your moral government, and he cannot be free to violate your dictates.

Just because your child is married doesn't mean that he can be disrespectful and expect to get away with it. Your children may be legal adults, but while they are in your house, you are the head of that house. If they refuse to submit to your leadership, they should be expected to pack their bags and move. Age has nothing to do with this important principle.

Adults are free to go where they want to go and to do what they want to do, but when they are depending on someone else for room and board, they lose a lot of liberties, and they are not totally their own bosses yet.

What they do when they are outside of your control is no longer your responsibility, and God will not hold you accountable for it — if you have been faithful to do what He has required of you in the home.

Christians can develop unity through:

- The demonstration of Christian love one to another
- The practical application of the Word of God
- Dedication to church and church activities
- Regular worship, including personal devotions, family altar, and public worship

Many families feel that they are "too busy" to take time for these unity-building activities. If that is true, they need to get their priorities straightened out. We can never be "too busy" to do the things that strengthen the family.

But you can't expect children to do nothing but pray and memorize Bible verses. God intended for His people to enjoy life, to enjoy each other, and to enjoy doing things together.

The family must be an exciting place to live and interact. Life doesn't have to be monotonous. Let the children be excited about participating in the special activities of the family, and they won't be so eager to go other places and do other things, things that often lead to their delinquency.

Plan activities for the whole family. Plan ahead, so that the children will have something to look forward to. Once a week, for example, schedule a family affair. Go to the beach and have a picnic with

The Foundation of Unity

the whole family. Do things together, things that are interesting to the children. Don't keep your children locked up inside the house all the time.

Once a month, plan some other wholesome activity for the whole family: camping, hiking, horseback riding, swimming, etc. You don't always have to do things that are expensive. Many very enjoyable activities don't cost much.

Take a little trip together, and take a lunch along. There are many interesting things to see and many things to learn. Learn about nature and about animals. These are things that interest children, and they are wholesome activities for the whole family.

In big cities, there are museums, zoos, amusement parks and many other such attractions that will catch the interest of children.

Nature is inspiring. It blesses anyone to see the marvels that God has created. And it won't hurt you, as parents, to learn something new as well.

Be resourceful and creative in these activities. Children are eager to see new things and to learn new things. Think of fun things that you can afford and that everyone will benefit from. Plan well, coordinate well, and leave plenty of time to enjoy everything. This is as important as any other responsibility you have.

After your children are grown, it becomes more and more difficult to gather them all together. Everyone has conflicting schedules. Those who are in college or those who have taken jobs have serious commitments that cannot be easily pushed aside to accommodate family gatherings. If you want everyone to attend some family gathering, advise them many months in advance so they can plan for it. Consult with them on their schedules and try to find a date that satisfies the needs of everyone.

Do whatever is necessary to maintain a team spirit in your home and with your family. As God is one, and His Church is one, let us be one in the marriage and one in the family, united by our one desire to honor God in everything that we do and say.

As a parent, you can never pass on your responsibility to others (for instance, to an older child for his or her younger brother or sister). You may ask others to contribute and to share some aspect of the child-rearing process, but you cannot deny your responsibility and pass it to others. I hate the mentality among our Filipino people that has caused them to rely on the oldest son or daughter to sacrifice and send the other brothers and sisters through school. By the time that oldest child has fulfilled his or her responsibility, he or she is too old to get married

The Foundation of Unity

and has to live the rest of his or her life alone. That is not fair.

It is also not fair to demand any service from your children, to demand that they support you, to demand that they do special favors for you. If they want to, that is different. But it is not right to demand it. God did not give us children for our benefit. We are given for their benefit. They are not our slaves. We are their servants, for the Lord's sake.

This habit of demanding things of our adult children destroys many marriages. When the in-laws demand support and the couple is struggling to keep their heads above water, it creates unfair strain upon the marriage.

That child did not ask to be born into this world. God gave you that child to care for. God gave you that child to nurture. God gave you that child as a holy, sublime responsibility and obligation. Do not try to turn that around. Care for your children. Educate your children. Raise up your children without expecting anything in return. If they remember you, thank God, but if they don't, thank God anyway. Your children owe you nothing. You have only done what was expected of you.

If they have been brought up in the right way, they cannot help but think of you when they are doing well. One day my youngest daughter and I were joking together. *What would happen to me,* we wondered, *when I was old, too old to travel, and alone in this world?*

"I wonder what it would be like in a nursing home," I said.

My daughter jumped up and said, "That will never happen, Dad. I will not get married, I will take care of you."

I said, "Darling, I know that won't be necessary. But just the thought of it makes me feel wonderful."

When we put demands on our children, they tighten with resistance. When we put none, they open up with compassion.

When you make demands on your wife, you will always meet resistance. But if you approach her with love, you will find her more than willing to meet your request.

If wives make demands on their husbands, they are putting wood to the fire, and there will be an explosion sooner or later. Use love, and you will get all that you want from them. Working together to develop a spirit of unity in the home will go a long way toward finding God's order for your family.

➜

Chapter 6

The Foundation of Love

Jesus said unto him, Thou shalt love the Lord thy God with all thy heart, and with all thy soul, and with all thy mind. This is the first and great commandment. And the second is like unto it, Thou shalt love thy neighbour as thyself. On these two commandments hang all the law and the prophets. Matthew 22:37-40

The greatest commandment is love and our nearest neighbors are the members of our own family. Therefore, they are the first people we must love.

The Apostle Paul wrote of love:

Love is patient, love is kind. It does not envy, it does not boast, it is not proud. It is not rude, it is not self-seeking, it is not easily angered, it keeps no record of wrongs. Love does not delight in evil but rejoices with the truth. It always protects,

*always trusts, always hopes, always perseveres.
Love never fails.*   1 Corinthians 13:4-8, NIV

LOVE! What a magic word! There is no more beautiful phrase in the world than, *I LOVE YOU,* and there is no more dreaded phrase in the world than, "It seems like my husband doesn't love me anymore." Love makes all the difference. Love, God's love, makes the world go round. It is the glue that holds the marriage and the family together.

A child who grows up in an atmosphere of love cannot help but love. And a child who grows up in an atmosphere of hate cannot help but hate. Love begets love, and hate begets hate.

Love is a two-way street. When a sister, in counseling, tells me that her husband doesn't seem to love her anymore, I ask her: "Have you told him that you love him recently?"

"No," she usually answers.

"Then, how can you expect to harvest, when you haven't planted?" I ask.

Love begets love. Love produces love. The husband will say, "Why do I need to tell her over and over again that I love her? I married her, didn't I? I have lived with her for five years, haven't I? If she doesn't know by now that I love her, she must be stupid."

The Foundation of Love

But, men, what good is it to love if that love is not expressed? Your wife is not a mind reader. She doesn't know everything you are thinking. You need to tell her.

Women, your husband can't read your mind. He needs to hear from you that you still love him, in spite of all his failings. Tell him.

The most terrible words a person can hear from the lips of a spouse is that dreadful phrase, "I don't love you anymore. I want a divorce." That hits you in the pit of the stomach. Nothing could be worse. I would rather die than hear those words. And, again, nothing could be better than knowing you are loved. Love makes all the difference.

Divorce is inevitable when a man and a woman fail to develop and sustain their love for one another. As unity in marriage is the result of allowing God's love to develop in us for each other, a lack of love leads to divorce. Everyone wants to be loved, and when a man or woman cannot find love in their marriage, they naturally begin to look elsewhere.

My own wife died, and the agony and pain her death caused me is indescribable, but I know from counseling with many people who have gone though a divorce that they have suffered far more than I.

It is unbearable to know that a man who once loved you is even now cradling another woman in his arms. You may even see them walking hand in hand and know that you should be the one he is holding. The agony of it! The pain of it! It seems to last forever.

And the devil will torment you and insist that it happened because you were not a good wife or husband. He will tell you, over and over again, "You are a failure. You are a failure. You are a failure. You drove your husband/your wife into the arms of another."

I know what I am talking about. I have counseled with many young people. I have seen cases of nineteen- or twenty-year-olds who had their lives already destroyed. They were ashamed to go out in public. They felt they couldn't hold their heads up. They were totally embarrassed by the failure of their marriage.

Many of the couples that are destroyed are left financially devastated and end up living on food stamps. They hate to buy anything at the grocery store because they don't want people to know how low they have fallen. What a tragedy!

Treasure the mate God has given you. Love them and let them know that you love them. We shouldn't

The Foundation of Love

wait until a person is at the point of death before we tell them how much we appreciate them. The Scriptures teach:

Render therefore to all their dues: tribute to whom tribute is due; custom to whom custom; fear to whom fear; honour to whom honour.

Romans 13:7

We are emotional beings and should not be afraid to release and reveal our emotions. Emotion is not made to be bottled up. It is made to demonstrate. It is unhealthy to suppress it. In certain cultures, we are taught never to show our emotions, to keep them hidden. This is not healthy for any individual of any nationality.

If you keep your emotions bottled up, they will eventually explode in a negative way. In the 50s and 60s, in our country, it was not very acceptable to see couples holding hands in public. The idea was to keep personal and intimate things in the bedroom and not to display them in public. To a certain degree, that thought had validity. But it is not wrong to express affection outside the bedroom, as long as it is proper.

In the countryside especially, we Filipinos were bound by this tradition, but now that is changing.

We realize that touching and holding hands is nothing obscene. It is good for us and good for our children to show them that we love one another. It is not wrong to kiss your husband or wife publicly. It is not wrong to hold each other tightly.

What will people think? Will they think we are immoral? I don't think so.

I still know couples who refuse to walk together. The husband goes ahead, and the wife follows him. To others, it appears that they barely know each other. When they go to the shopping center, he does his shopping, and she does her shopping. You don't know if they have a healthy relationship or not. You don't know if they speak to each other at home or not. What they are doing is not healthy. Something seems to be very wrong. The situation smells of trouble.

My thought would be, *I wonder if they had a fight before they came* or *I wonder if they are about to divorce.* Let us cast off every mold into which Satan tries to place us.

At the same time, we must be morally upright in our conduct. It is never acceptable for us to become fresh and vulgar in a public place. Restaurants have to send couples out sometimes because they are offending the patrons. That is never correct. You

The Foundation of Love

can show affection and release intimate affections without being offensive.

Some couples never show any kind of affection in front of their children. Some children are grown and can say, "I have never seen my father kiss or embrace my mother." As a result, they think that this is the correct way for husbands and wives to relate to each other.

You fathers can do nothing greater for your children than to love their mother and express your love for her openly. It is healthy for the children to see that you appreciate the woman who is the most important and wonderful woman in the world to them. They will say, "That is the kind of marriage I would like to have." But when they see you fighting like cats and dogs, it will have just the opposite effect.

I have a friend that I pushed to get married. "Why are you pushing me?" he asked.

"Because you are not getting any younger. Why don't you want to get married?" I said.

"Why should I get married?" he answered, "I watched my mother and father, how they treated each other, and I don't want to live like that."

I understand exactly what he was saying. We should show forth a good example of God's love to others, especially to our own children.

Just touching each other is a powerful testimony. And touch is a very powerful way to demonstrate our love. Touch can be electrifying. There are tiny nerves in our skin that are sensitive to touch. Everyone likes to be touched. There are many emotions that can be transmitted through touching.

When we study the life of Jesus, we find that ninety percent of His ministry involved touching. He touched people. Touch is reassuring. Touch is reaffirming. Touch is encouraging. That is why, when someone is upset and you hug them tightly, the bad feelings pass and they feel secure. Our spouses need our loving touch.

Love can be expressed in understanding. Just as every husband feels the need of an understanding and submissive wife, every wife needs an understanding and cooperative husband. I find this to be a particular need among women.

My opinion is that the women are the most in need of understanding in the home. They are overloaded with thankless tasks. When husbands and wives enjoy each other physically, the wife bears the burden and pain of childbearing as a result. When your child is born, it is usually the wife who wakes up early to tend to the child. Usually it is the mother who takes the child to sports and music lessons and to

The Foundation of Love

the doctor's office for checkups and shots. She cooks the meals, cleans the house and washes clothes. And she can't count on working nine to five. Her work is twenty-four hours a day, seven days a week. What a great responsibility!

Nowadays, the majority of women also work outside the home to bring in added income. This only increases their load. They do the outside work and still have their own personal responsibilities waiting for them when they get home. They are still expected to do the major share of the household chores. But marriage is a partnership and husbands must take their share of the load. If not, the wife will quickly feel that she is being taken advantage of and used like a slave rather than a true partner in marriage.

When her husband comes home from his work, she says, "Dear, I have to help Suzie with her homework. Could you wash the dishes for me?" The husband, instead, falls into the rocking chair, claiming that he is "just too tired" to do it. He is sure she will understand. Yes, she understands that he is tired; but she is twice as tired, and he needs to understand that. We want the women to do all the understanding, but they need some understanding too.

Once I said to my wife, "Honey, I got a revelation from God."

"What is it?" she asked.

"I feel sorry for wives," I said. "They are full-time employees without a salary."

In reality, most wives are not looking for financial payment. They are looking for a little understanding, a little kindness, a little encouragement, a little assurance, a little appreciation.

A major study of employees in a broad range of jobs showed that more people are looking for a little appreciation from their employers than a raise or an advancement. We all need to be appreciated.

I have found that when wives get a little bit of understanding, they are willing to serve their families faithfully. Be understanding, husbands; be appreciative. That is not asking too much of you.

I learned this lesson the hard way, by experience. As long as I was taking my wife for granted and was demanding that she understand my position, I watched her shrivel up like a prune, becoming irritable and impatient and fairly unbearable to live with. When I learned the importance of showing her more understanding and appreciation, I watched her blossom. She became more supportive of me, and I got more response from her. A little understanding makes all the difference in the world.

The Foundation of Love

When I applied the medication of a little understanding, taking time to touch my wife and to voice my appreciation of her, everything changed in my personal life. I only wished I had leaned the lesson earlier.

"Darling, what could I ever do without you?" Such simple words, but how true! And all women love to hear that. (If any of them say they don't, they are deceiving themselves.) We all long to be appreciated.

Love causes us to see things from the other person's perspective, to understand where they are coming from, to see their viewpoint — although it may be very different from our own.

Without love, there can be no understanding, because applying understanding requires some sacrifice on our part. It is an unselfish act, and when you do it, it shows maturity; it shows that you are leaving self-centeredness and entering spouse-centeredness.

God, who is the Head of the Church, fully understands the humanity of every member of His Church. He is, therefore, not harsh with any of us. He is not impatient with any of us. He is not judgmental with any of us. He knows the limitations of human beings.

In the same loving way, you must also understand the limitations and the weaknesses of every member of the family. It is as God's love flows from the Head to the sub-head, the father, and from him to the other members of the family, that we can all experience God's love in our marriages and in our family life in general. It can only come about through God's love.

God is love:

And we have known and believed the love that God hath to us. God is love; and he that dwelleth in love dwelleth in God, and God in him.

1 John 4:16

So, if God is in you, you can demonstrate His love to your spouse and to your family.

God demonstrated His love for us by giving us His Son:

For God so loved the world, that he gave his only begotten Son, that whosoever believeth in him should not perish, but have everlasting life.

John 3:16

Love must be demonstrated. God knew that we could not make it without Him. In the same way, the husband should love his wife and his family and give himself sacrificially for them. In fact, the

The Foundation of Love

Scriptures teach us that we should love our wives *"as Christ loved the Church."*

> *Husbands, love your wives, even as Christ also loved the church, and gave himself for it;*
> Ephesians 5:25

That is a BIG order! Christ *"gave himself for"* the Church. Husbands, don't expect too much of your wife. God has given YOU the supreme responsibility in the home. Your wife needs you to love her, to support her, to protect her, to understand her and to reassure her. We were married nineteen years before my wife died, and, in those nineteen years, I found that my wife often needed reassurance of my love for her.

If you have a hard time saying, "I love you," buy your wife some chocolate candy. If you have difficulty saying "I love you," buy her some roses. If you have difficulty saying "I love you," wash the dishes for her. If you have difficulty saying "I love you," cook the meal and have it ready when she gets home. If you have difficulty saying "I love you," take her out for a ride. Actions are always better than words anyway.

When the foundation of love is securely in place, you can expect God to work on your behalf. Many of the tragedies we experience come about as a result of broken and crippled relationships. When we have a great need as a family or as a couple, the first thing we should always do is to check to see how our relationship is doing. If it needs some restoration, that is the first order of business. Restore the proper relationship between the various members of the family, and, I promise you, God will bless you and supply your every need.

You may need physical healing. You may have a great financial need. And you may be wondering what, if anything, this has to do with how well you get along with your spouse and your children. I want to tell you that it has everything to do with how well you get along with your spouse and children. God cannot bless you if you are constantly squabbling among yourselves. God cannot bless you if you are failing to show His love to those closest to you. Prosperity in your home begins with finding God's order for your family.

Love helps you develop a positive, healthy attitude so that you will not react wrongly in a tense situation. A lot of our problems come from the action and reaction that begins with insignificant little things and leads to marital and family tragedy. It is very important how you react to your spouse and

The Foundation of Love

your children. And God wants to help you learn to always have a loving response.

When marital argument become serious, husbands and wives often cannot even remember what led to the argument. All they can remember are the accusations and recriminations that hurt them so much and lead to further bad reactions on their part. When they finally do remember what started it all, they are startled to realize that it was something of nearly zero significance. But one bad reaction after another builds on that insignificant thing, until a real rupture is imminent.

It might go like this:

> *"Why isn't dinner ready? I'm hungry!"*
> *"I haven't had time to cook yet."*
> *"What do you mean you haven't cooked yet? That is your responsibility! What do you do with all your time, anyway?"*
> *"I just got busy taking care of YOUR children and forgot the time."*
> *"You are my wife, and it is your place to cook and have my meals ready on time, when I want them. Now, I have to go out and my dinner isn't ready. Do you think that is right?"*

Can you see the steam building? This is a very typical scene. This could all be avoided very easily. If the wife would say, "I'm sorry! I got busy and wasn't able to get the meal ready in time," then the husband might answer, "Oh, that's okay. Let me fix something quickly for us both. It's my turn to cook anyway." He might even want to order out or to take her out for a meal.

In another common scenario, the husband arrives to find his wife sitting on the couch. He begins the conversation:

> *"Honey, I'm hungry."*
> *"The food is on the table. I heard you coming and warmed it up for you."*
> *"Honey, didn't you hear me? I'm hungry!"*
> *"The food is on the table. What more do you want?"*
> *"Well, then, let's eat. What are we waiting for? I'm hungry."*
> *"I ate already. You were late, and I was hungry. So I went ahead and ate."*
> *"Why couldn't you wait for me? You always wait for me. We always eat together."*
> *"I was hungry."*

The Foundation of Love

"Now you're making me lose my appetite. We always eat together. I don't feel right eating without you. We don't have enough time together. Come on. Let's sit down together."

"Beans? You know that I don't like beans."

"Well, if you don't want beans, don't eat the beans."

"I won't eat them. You eat beans if you like beans so well."

Can you sense the steam building up here? It doesn't take a great imagination to think what might happen next, does it? With each action, there is a more violent reaction.

What might have changed this atmosphere? Well, if the wife had eaten something light in order to be able to sit down and enjoy a meal with her man when he got home, he might not have rejected her beans.

This whole episode began because both husband and wife were tired and hungry. These are the silly little situations that Satan takes advantage of to destroy us. In love, you must be careful to always respond with the correct attitude. If your attitude is not right, it is better to bite your tongue and say nothing at all. Sour produces sour. Recrimination produces recrimination. Just learning how to bite your tongue will go a long way toward preventing World War III in your home.

The wise King Solomon declared:

A soft answer turneth away wrath: but grievous words stir up anger. Proverbs 15:1

Just swallow those words. Don't bother to utter them out loud. Too many times we talk without even thinking about what we are saying. We say foolish things that hurt our spouses and create an atmosphere of contention. And, as a result, the war is on.

We are much too quick to speak and much too slow to evaluate what we say. Evaluate before you speak, and you will keep yourself out of a lot of trouble. Silence is golden. It may even keep you out of the dog house.

We will one day be held accountable for what we say. Jesus said:

For by thy words thou shalt be justified, and by thy words thou shalt be condemned.
Matthew 12:37

Some people are facing a terrible condemnation because of the loose way in which they throw words

The Foundation of Love

around! Be understanding. Instead of responding to the reaction of your spouse or your children, stop to analyze the cause for that response. Do not attack the symptoms of the problem. Go to the root of the problem.

Wives, sometimes you can get further with your husband with hugs than you can with nagging. Husbands need to be hugged more. They don't need to be nagged.

Husbands, maybe your wife is feeling insecure. At that moment, she doesn't need you to insult her. She needs to be held tightly in your arms and to feel your strength and love. If you will just wrap her in your arms, the insecurity will pass, and she will be reassured.

Men, hear what I am saying. I know what I am talking about. Do not be afraid to show your emotions to your wife. Do not be afraid to express your love for her. Many husbands are so reserved when they are around their wives, afraid to open up to them and be vulnerable. But those same men are totally open with their secretaries and female co-workers. Why is that?

One of the reasons men do this is that they have gotten too many negative reactions from their wives and fear that if they open up to them it will happen again. That puts the wife in an awkward position, too. She doesn't know where her husband is coming from. She doesn't know what he is thinking or what he is feeling. Don't let this happen to your most important earthly relationships. Never be afraid to say, "Honey, I love you."

Your wife may be furious with you for some reason or other. She may be just waiting for you to come home so that she can lambaste you good for some infraction of the rules, real or imagined. But when you come home with a big smile and with expressions of love, all will be forgiven and forgotten. Love melts all anger. Love melts hatred and resentment. Love melts negative emotions. If you come home with this loving attitude, you will get the positive response you are looking for. If your own attitude is loving and healthy, chances are that it will evoke a loving and healthy response from your spouse.

If we understand this truth, we can prevent so many of the major upsets we have all experienced in the home. But, when we marry, we are so young, so naive, so ignorant of the intricate workings of a man or a woman, that we do many foolish things.

During the first few days of the honeymoon, we are floating on air. Oh, the emotion! Oh, the thrill! Oh, the excitement! But, when our feet hit the floor,

The Foundation of Love

what a shock it is! It nearly gives us a heart attack. "Oh, my," we think, "What have I gotten myself into? What an idiot I was to make such a serious commitment without understanding what I was getting myself into!"

But, as we begin to learn to understand each other, our imaginations are broadened and our horizons expanded, until we come to find that a woman is a woman, and a man is a man and the chemical make-up and the emotional needs of each are totally different. And we are on our way to understanding and appreciating each other, as different as we might be.

The most serious complaints of wives all over the world against their husbands are all basically the same:

"My husband is no longer giving me the attention I need from him."
"My husband is taking me for granted. He doesn't appreciate what I do for him."

I have heard it over and over in my counseling sessions as a pastor:

"He has time for his buddies at the baseball field. He has time to go fishing with his friends. Before

we got married, he thought he absolutely could not live without me. But since we got married, he spends more time with his friends than he does with me. He only wants to sleep with me from time to time. He doesn't seem to need me for anything else."

"He rushes home from work, takes a quick shower and gets a quick bite to eat, and goes right out again to be with his friends. If I ask him to stay home and help me because I'm not feeling well, he acts like I have deprived him of the right to live. His happiness is all that matters. He takes me totally for granted. What I feel or need is not important to him anymore."

Do you see what I am talking about? It doesn't take a lot of effort to turn a situation like this around, and what does it cost you? Nothing! You have everything to gain and nothing to lose from making every effort to do it. Demonstrate Christ-like love in your home consistently, and be blessed.

All of these foundations — the foundation of agreement, the foundation of unity, and the foundation of love — are interrelated. They all work together to produce and maintain a balanced and healthy relationship, one in which order reigns

The Foundation of Love

and in which peace and harmony produce beautiful music. What a joy it is to produce beautiful music!

A choir, in which all the voices blend together, is pleasant to listen to. I am not a music student, but I know what sounds good, and disharmony is hard to take.

When a musical instrument is well tuned, it brings forth something beautiful. When David played his harp, all the evil spirits departed from King Saul. When the musicians and singers joined together to praise God in the Temple, the glory of God came down. There is something very beautiful about harmony, about unity.

This beauty is what God has envisioned for your home. He has destined you to understand and work together with your spouse and with your children (instead of striving against each other) to create some beautiful music. This brings Him glory.

"I love you!"

It is not in how we say the words, it is how we live them. Love is an action. It must be demonstrated. You can't see it, you can't smell it, you can't feel it, you can't hear it. It must be demonstrated.

Love is an explosion, far beyond emotion. Emotion alone is not a proper basis for love.

Founded On the Rock

Love is a decision. You make up your mind that you are going to love, whether you feel like it or not. Because of this, love is not affected by the situation in which you find yourself. You love, in spite of the circumstances.

Love is a determination. You allow it to be born, then you water it with care and cultivate it with the knowledge that it will produce a godly harvest. It doesn't just happen by accident. Love is planted with sharing; it is watered with giving; and, in time, it blooms.

There is a BIG difference between love and lust. There is a BIG difference between a consuming passion and a sincere, honest, true love. What we do demonstrates our understanding of the facts.

Laying firmly the foundation of love will go a long way toward finding God's order for your family.

➜

Part III

Building upon Your Foundation

CHAPTER 7

COMMITMENT

The LORD is my shepherd; I shall not want. He maketh me to lie down in green pastures: he leadeth me beside the still waters. He restoreth my soul: he leadeth me in the paths of righteousness for his name's sake. Yea, though I walk through the valley of the shadow of death, I will fear no evil: for thou art with me; thy rod and thy staff they comfort me. Thou preparest a table before me in the presence of mine enemies: thou anointest my head with oil; my cup runneth over. Surely goodness and mercy shall follow me all the days of my life: and I will dwell in the house of the LORD for ever.

Psalm 23:1-6

We have now laid a wonderful foundation for a unique structure called *marriage*. We have laid the foundation for a unique God-inspired structure called *the home*. And those are good foundations. But foundations are not enough to build a complete structure. A finished building needs some supporting walls and a roof.

We now want to finish our structure with three elements which are just as important in the home as they are in the marriage: **commitment, contentment, and consistency**. Let us begin with commitment.

Commitment means: *to commit something to another, to turn it over, to allow yourself to be governed, to be ruled, giving yourself over to be controlled by another.* That may sound terrible to many of our modern individual rights-oriented people, but it is not terrible. It is wonderful. You give yourselves to each other for mutual benefit.

David, for instance, made a commitment to God. He would be God's sheep, and God would be his Shepherd. The relationship proved to be mutually satisfying. David could later say, *"I will fear no evil: for Thou art with me."*

David didn't lose anything by committing his life to God. He gained everything. Commitment is not a terrible thing, it is a wonderful thing.

David had no fears in life — because he had made a commitment. He had no needs in life — because he had made a commitment. He was not worried about the future — because he had made a commitment. He had every right to receive all of God's blessings

Commitment

— because he had made a commitment. You can have nothing without a corresponding commitment.

We like to go about things the wrong way. We want the benefits of commitment without making the actual commitment; and that simply doesn't work. When we read the 23rd Psalm, our attention is drawn to the phrase: *"I shall not want."* We like that phrase.

We like the fact that the Lord has promised to provide our every need. We like the fact that we need not worry about the future because "the Lord will supply." We rejoice in the blessing of God and in His prosperity. But what we usually don't see is that it is impossible to receive the blessings of the Shepherd if we fail to make a commitment to be one of His sheep.

David could say, *"I shall not want,"* because he had already made the commitment: *"The LORD is my shepherd."* His commitment changed everything. The benefits come with the commitment.

The benefits of the relationship are important, but they cannot be realized until the relationship is cemented. They cannot be realized if there is no commitment.

Furthermore, a healthy relationship is never based on the benefits we can derive from it. We don't make friends just so we can borrow things from them or ask them to help us with a project around the house. They are our friends. The benefits flow out of the relationship, not the other way around.

Those who only get married for sex are always disappointed with the relationship they have with their spouse. What you can get from the relationship is not a proper foundation for a relationship. Commitment to a relationship must come first. Any and all benefits will follow that commitment.

When you are genuinely committed to a person, you don't worry about what you can gain from the relationship. Rather, you are thinking more about what you can contribute to the relationship, how you can help the person to whom you have committed your life.

In making a commitment to the Lord, between Shepherd and sheep, you forfeit your own rights and submit yourself to His will — which you can be assured is always better than your own.

Therefore, you actually have no more rights. You actually have no more personal identity. You have made a commitment to someone else, and your identity is tied up in them. You are identified with Christ. *The LORD is my Shepherd* implies **I am His sheep**.

Commitment

When we preach the Gospel, we tell people, "Trust the Lord. Give your life to God. Make Him the Lord and Savior, and He will supply and provide all of your needs." And that is correct. But it is only half of the truth. People need to hear the rest of the Gospel.

I had preached this passage perhaps two hundred times when, one day, the Lord rebuked me and gave me a beautiful revelation: In order for us to receive the fullness of the blessing that the Shepherd has for us, we must establish that relationship by fully committing ourselves to Him.

The full truth is: The Lord is my Shepherd, and I am His sheep. When we emphasize only one side of the relationship, we lose the balance of the full commitment.

This relationship is not based only on everything that the Shepherd does for the sheep. The sheep do not have an exclusive right to reap all the benefit of the relationship. This relationship is two-sided. This is a mutually beneficial agreement, and we must do our part to make it work properly. Without our commitment to the relationship there can be no benefits.

The sheep and the shepherd must move together. That means the shepherd must be willing to lead, and the sheep must be willing to follow. The two form a unit that cannot go anywhere unless there is a mutual commitment to the roles that each is to play in the relationship and mutual understanding of those roles.

Until this is achieved, we cannot move into those *green pastures*. Until this is achieved, we will never know those *still waters*. The many promises of the relationship remain just that, promises, until a full commitment is made to accept and abide by the structure of the relationship.

The shepherd can guide the sheep into green pastures only if the sheep are willing to submit to his leadership and his control. That often does not happen because, as we all know, sheep have a mind and a will of their own. Unless the will of the sheep can be overcome, unless the mind of the sheep can be changed, he is doomed to lose the benefits of the shepherd's care. If the sheep and the shepherd are working against each other, rather than for each other, both will lose.

In the same way, a young man and a young woman, as they embark upon a new life together, must have a total change in their way of thinking, a change based on their total commitment to a new life together.

Commitment

Their old way of thinking, based on their own personal desires and tastes, must give way to a new way of thinking that contemplates the welfare of the entire family unit. You agree on the common good and begin to walk with a united purpose. You place yourselves in one mind for mutual benefit. In that moment, you take on a new identity. It is fully proper that the minister, at the close of the wedding ceremony, make the new couple known to the congregation, presenting them formally as Mr. & Mrs. _____ , for they are, indeed, a new entity. Two have become one, as the Scriptures declare:

> *Therefore shall a man leave his father and his mother, and shall cleave unto his wife: and they shall be one flesh.* Genesis 2:24
>
> *Wherefore they are no more twain, but one flesh. What therefore God hath joined together, let not man put asunder.* Matthew 19:6
> *And they twain shall be one flesh: so then they are no more twain, but one flesh.* Mark 10:8

What takes place in marriage is a miracle of God. Two individuals, sometimes two very different individuals, are joined into one unit. Two minds merge. Two hearts merge. The fleshly merging is not the important one. The flesh can be united without the uniting of mind and heart. If hearts and minds are not joined, the two are still going in different directions in life, and the results can only be tragic.

The Shepherd is committed to supplying the needs of the sheep. The Shepherd is committed to protecting the sheep. The Shepherd is committed to guide and direct the sheep. But, unless the sheep are wiling to commit their lives to follow and obey the direction and the guidance of the Shepherd, they will be lost and will never receive any of that promised provision.

When the wife is willing to say, "I am yours, I think no longer of my own desire and of my own pleasure in life, I live only to provide your pleasure and delight," that is the basis for a relationship that will last through all of life's storms.

When the husband realizes that the consuming passion of his life is no longer to achieve his own enjoyment, his own satisfaction, his own fulfillment, but that of the one he loves, that is the basis for a relationship that will not be easily destroyed, come what may.

Our old way of thinking must be reversed. The sheep cannot be thinking only of himself; he must be thinking of the shepherd. The shepherd cannot

Commitment

be thinking of himself and his own welfare; he must be thinking of the sheep.

What a powerful truth this brings us for the marriage and the home. Wives, when you stop thinking only of yourself and, husbands, when you stop thinking only of yourself, a beautiful relationship will result.

If you insist on being selfish and self-centered, either of you, I promise you nothing. You can look forward to disappointment, hurt, anger, and loss.

If Christian wives continue to insist on making all their own decisions and on dominating the home and not giving the man of the house a chance to lead, I cannot promise that you will be blessed.

If you don't like the decisions your husband is making, pray for him. The Scriptures teach us:

> *I exhort therefore, that, first of all, supplications, prayers, intercessions, and giving of thanks, be made for all men; For kings, and for all that are in authority; that we may lead a quiet and peaceable life in all godliness and honesty.*
>
> 1 Timothy 2:1-2

It may seem out of context to some to relate this passage to marriage and the home, but I don't see it that way. I believe that the home is the very context in which all authority must begin. We pray for the president; we pray for the governors; we pray for our mayors. We pray for all those who are in authority, except the men who are in authority in our homes, the basic unit of society.

Wife, your husband has been given by God the responsibility to govern his home. He is responsible for the direction it takes. He is responsible for its protection and for its spiritual and physical welfare. Don't work against him; work with him to achieve those goals.

Many would like to change that God-given order in the home. But it was not chauvinistic on God's part to give the man authority. It was His desire to establish order out of chaos. When we follow God's order, His Word, He can bless us. When everyone is going his or her own way, we tie the hands of God.

Husbands, start taking your responsibilities seriously. Start doing what you have committed yourself to do, and the response of your family members will be more encouraging. Your commitment to love your wife *"as Christ loved the Church"* has nothing to do with sex or how you might feel at the moment. It has nothing to do with how your partner might be behaving. Christ loves the Church, regardless of any

Commitment

other circumstance. His love is without reservation.

Peter expressed it well in his first letter to the churches:

> *Likewise, ye husbands, dwell with them according to knowledge, giving honour unto the wife, as unto the weaker vessel, and as being heirs together of the grace of life; that your prayers be not hindered.*
> 1 Peter 3:7

You are *"heirs together,"* but the larger responsibility is clearly upon the man. He is to *"give honour unto the wife, as unto the weaker vessel."* That certainly doesn't make her any less, but it places upon his shoulders the heavier load. If this commitment is not honored, warns the Lord, your prayers will be *"hindered."*

What most men don't seem to realize is that after the two have become one, and he comes to hate his wife and mistreats her, he is hating and mistreating himself:

> *So ought men to love their wives as their own bodies. He that loveth his wife loveth himself. For no man ever yet hated his own flesh; but nourisheth and cherisheth it, even as the Lord the church: For*

we are members of his body, of his flesh, and of his bones. For this cause shall a man leave his father and mother, and shall be joined unto his wife, and they two shall be one flesh. This is a great mystery: but I speak concerning Christ and the church.

Ephesians 5:28-32

These are not my words. These are God's words.

Wives don't seem to realize that when they defy their husbands and constantly try to pull the wool over his eyes, they are only hurting themselves. Submitting to his leadership will not hurt you. It will help you. Being a dutiful wife is not old-fashioned and out of date. It is the current necessity. It is the wise thing to do, for you and for your children. It is the only way in which you can build a happy home.

That doesn't make you anything less. As I said in an earlier chapter, the husband is the legislative branch of the government of the home. He gives direction and sets up the laws. The wife is the executive branch of the family. She carries out the direction that is communicated to her.

Wives, you are given to your husband as his helpmeet. Help him; don't work against him. You are in this thing together. This is a team effort. Don't work against your most important teammate.

Commitment

God has given us the example of how the family team should work. As God, He doesn't really need our help, but He has given us the privilege of being His co-workers, nevertheless:

> *We then, as workers together with him, beseech you also that ye receive not the grace of God in vain.*   2 Corinthians 6:1

Husbands and wives are *"workers together"* in the home, co-workers in our modern way of speaking. You are co-workers in maintaining peace and order and harmony within your home. You are co-workers in the development of your children and their particular talents. You are co-workers in the teaching and accompanying discipline that is an integral part of any successful home. And all of this takes a serious commitment on your part.

When both partners make a full commitment to the marriage, you have more than a 50-50 relationship. Since each of the partners is giving 100 percent, you have a 200 percent investment, and, therefore you have double the potential.

Marriage is better than 100 percent. It is 200 percent. Both partners are giving everything. That's why the Scriptures say that *"two are better than one"*:

Two are better than one; because they have a good reward for their labour. For if they fall, the one will lift up his fellow: but woe to him that is alone when he falleth; for he hath not another to help him up. Again, if two lie together, then they have heat: but how can one be warm alone? And if one prevail against him, two shall withstand him; and a threefold cord is not quickly broken.

Ecclesiastes 4:9-12

The men of Moses time knew the strength that comes with uniting our hearts in total commitment. One, it was said could *"chase a thousand,"* but two, it was declared, could *"put ten thousand to flight"* (Deuteronomy 32:30).

When you make a total commitment, the result is loyalty, fidelity, faithfulness, submission, surrender, and acknowledgment of position and function within the family.

For better or for worse.
For richer or for poorer.
In sickness and in health ...
Cleaving only unto thee
... until death do us part.

Commitment

That slams the door behind us. We have made an absolute, total, and definite commitment. When that commitment is made and kept you are on your way to developing an indestructible relationship. You are on your way to finding God's order for your family.

➜

Chapter 8

Contentment

Not that I speak in respect of want: for I have learned, in whatsoever state I am, therewith to be content.   Philippians 4:11

What does it mean to be content? Someone has said, jokingly, that Contentment is the best state in the whole United States. They were right. Maybe you didn't know that the Apostle Paul traveled in North America. Well, this verse is the proof. He was happy in whatever *state* he was in.

Seriously, now: What is contentment? The word means *to be fulfilled, happy, or satisfied.*

When you are content, you are complete. You are not looking for something else to satisfy you. None of the ingredients of life are missing. You are at peace, you are happy, you are satisfied, you are comfortable, you are fulfilled, you are relaxed, you are at rest, you have peace of mind.

Contentment

As Christians, our contentment must not be affected by outside influences. Many people are just like the weather, very changeable. When it is cloudy and rains, they are dreary. When the sun is shining, they are smiling. When it is winter, they are cold; and when it is summer they are hot. These people are moody, and their mood changes, depending on the circumstances around them.

A contented person has an inner peace that is not destroyed by what happens from day to day. Whatever happens, he or she is still happy.

People who lack contentment in life are grumblers, murmurers, and complainers. They always have a sour attitude. Beautiful things look ugly to them. Bright things look gloomy to them. Nothing makes them happy; nothing satisfies them.

A person who is contented can eat the simplest food and be happy with it, but nothing pleases a grumbler.

God is looking for a contented people. A contented person is a gracious person, a beaming person, a rejoicing person. Paul said:

Rejoice in the Lord alway: and again I say, Rejoice.
                                             Philippians 4:4

Sometimes it is easy to rejoice. When everything is going well, anyone can rejoice. But Paul is teaching us to *rejoice always,* in every state, in every circumstance in which we find ourselves. And that is not as easy, is it?

Some ladies might ask, "Do you mean to say that even if my husband didn't come home on time yesterday, I should rejoice?"

Yes, that is exactly what I am saying. And that is exactly what Paul teaches. He says we are to rejoice *"in all things."*

> *Be careful for nothing; but in every thing by prayer and supplication with thanksgiving let your requests be made known unto God.* Philippians 4:6

> *In every thing give thanks: for this is the will of God in Christ Jesus concerning you.*
> 1 Thessalonians 5:18

The reason Paul can tell us to rejoice in everything is that God is good and is working everything out for the good of those who love Him.

> *And we know that all things work together for good to them that love God, to them who are the called according to his purpose.* Romans 8:28

Contentment

Another might ask, "Do you mean to say that if my husband has a date with his secretary, I should rejoice?"

Yes, strangely enough, that is what I mean. I am not saying that it is a good thing for your husband to stray. Don't misunderstand me. I am saying that if you get excited about your experience in the Lord and become an excited and exciting person, a person full of joy and life, your husband will be much less likely to stray from home.

Another might ask, "Do you mean to say that even though we are financially broke I should rejoice?"

Yes, strangely enough, that is what I mean, and that is what the Bible is teaching us. Although being broke cannot be termed a good or a pleasant experience, your murmuring and complaining can't change the situation. And, if you have to be broke, it is better to be happy about it. It is better to be a happy broke person than a miserable broke person.

Contentment is a wonderful thing. It has the power to change the circumstances of your life. And contentment is never based on physical circumstances. It is not based on the accumulation of physical things. It must be based entirely on the commitment we have made to God and to each other.

Just as we can rejoice in the midst of trials because we know that God is working out everything for our good, we can be content in our marriage, knowing that our love and commitment will, in the end, enable us to overcome any differences that might arise from time to time. As believers, we can have that assurance.

Christians should be content with their situation in life, but I know Christians who are moved by every circumstance. They are on cloud nine when the blessings are flowing in their lives. They are the first to jump up and testify during those times. However, the first moment that things do not go well for them, they are ready to backslide. They cannot praise the Lord when it is raining. They are silent when things are not to their liking. Maybe we should call them fair-weather believers. They have victory only in good times.

True believers, people of faith in an unchanging God, always have the victory. They can praise God in the most difficult of times, because they know that He never changes, and that whatever the circumstances may be, God is still God and still holds the whole world in His hands. We need more of these genuinely contented believers. And marriages would benefit from more contented spouses.

Contentment

We have a saying in the Philippines: *"A shallow river is a noisy river, but a deep river runs silent."* The greater your commitment to each other, the less you will be grumbling and complaining. The deeper your commitment to each other and to your family, the happier you will be.

You must realize that your commitment to each other is a commitment to God. So, if you accept the fact of being where God has placed you and accept the circumstances under which He has chosen to let you operate, I guarantee you that the blessing and prosperity of God and the abundant supply of the Lord will never pass your door. It will flow in until there is no more place to receive it.

The Shepherd is committed to lead us into green pastures, to take us beside the still waters, to make us sit down at the banqueting table. Let us be content to follow Him. He is committed to restoring your soul. Be content to let Him do it. He is committed to having you sit at His banqueting table. Be content to eat what He has prepared for you.

With faith in His goodness, accept your lot in life and begin to make the best of your situation. Know that your spouse is God's gift to you and that your children are God's gift to you. Love them and be content with them, and God will bless you for it.

When you start showing your love for each other, there will be no room for gloomy days, for total commitment will bring total contentment. It is not enough to be content one day. Be content every day. And when you become satisfied and content, God will move on your behalf.

We have been led to believe that our happiness depends on the actions of our spouse, but that is not true. Our happiness and fulfillment depend on the depth of our commitment and nothing else. If we are unwilling to make a full commitment, our spouses can do all the right things, and we will still not be happy.

When our commitment is deep, nothing can shake us. Even if we are poor, we feel rich. Even if we are sick, we feel well. Even if we have problems, we feel free. Nothing shakes our sense of well-being.

Most married people are happy if all the bills are paid, if they have a nice home, if they have a new car, if there are some savings in the bank. But many become restless when the bill collector is at the door, when the landlord threatens eviction, when the light company sends a cutoff notice, or when the bank sends a foreclosure statement.

They begin to blame each other. It sounds something like this:

Contentment

"If you weren't such a lazy husband, we wouldn't be in this trouble."

"If you weren't such an extravagant spender, we would be able to pay our bills."

"Why don't you get more overtime?"

"Why don't you concentrate on buying only what we need?"

"Oh, honey, it's on sale."

"Even if it's on sale, we don't need it. And if we don't need it, it's a waste of money. It would just sit around here and collect dust. So, even if it's cheap, don't buy it."

If you are committed to your mate and to your family, you will know that everyone passes through some rough times, and you won't blame each other when those moments come. You will join together in prayer for God's help, and you will support each other in every trial and test. Most of all, you will be content — even in the difficult circumstances.

If you are content to let the Lord be your Shepherd, you will not want. If you insist on being the shepherd, you will go hungry. If you are content to let Him lead, He will take you beside those still waters. If you insist on leading yourself, you will get hopelessly lost. Sheep are not capable of knowing the way. Sheep wander away and lose their sense of direction.

If you are content to let the Shepherd lead you into those green pastures, you will find a place of rest. If you continue to rebel against His will and refuse to be content with His best for your life, your end will be sad.

When you refuse to be content with your spouse, you are refusing the will of God, because your spouse is your special gift from Him. Will you reject His choice for your life? Will you despise His taste and think that you know better?

Contentment does not come through having everything that you want in life. Contentment comes through having everything that He wants for you. Contentment does not come through the accumulation of goods. It comes through a serious commitment to the will of God and to each other.

One of our greatest tests as a couple and as a family came when we left our country to be missionaries to Guam. We had been serving for five years in the ministry team of the largest church in Southeast Asia, Bethel Temple of Manila (in the days before the church of Paul Yonggi Cho in Seoul, Korea, grew so large). We were very comfortable and secure in our position. We had a free apartment and a good

Contentment

salary. The people loved us and gave us special gifts every Sunday and Wednesday. We rarely had to buy groceries. We were well taken care of. But God was dealing with our hearts to launch out into a greater work.

Since our mission did not want us to leave, and since they had no mission program for Filipinos, they could not help us either with our passage or with our monthly support.

The Lord provided our airline tickets, and we sensed that it was time for us to go, regardless of the lack of guarantee for our daily sustenance. We landed in Guam with only $54 in our pockets. There were three of us, my wife and myself and our fourteen-month-old daughter, Joy.

We looked around for a place to stay in Guam and finally landed in an old house four miles from the airport. The rent was $12 a month. It was in such bad shape that no one had lived there for many years. The only inhabitants were pigeons. The place hadn't been cleaned for so long that the dust, in places, was three inches thick.

The house sat on stilts, but it was tilted, and two of the posts were off the ground. When you walked through the house, everything creaked, as if the floor would give way at any minute. So we walked carefully.

Founded On the Rock

There was no way to close the windows. They were just open holes in the wall. At night, the mosquitoes came through those holes in battle strength. They were so big and so vicious that I almost expected to see them with helmets and combat boots.

There was no furniture in the house. We had one towel and one sheet, our clothes, and not much more. That would have to do us until some boxes that we had shipped arrived. We found a bundle of yellowed, mildewed newspapers. I took one from the middle of the stack and spread it on the floor, put the sheet over it, and that was our bed. We got ready and went to "bed."

Before long, we heard a sound and thought that someone was coming in to rob us. It was only some rats. They were big ones. We lay back down and tried to sleep, but we couldn't. The mosquitoes seemed to have loud speakers. They came in like kamikaze dive bombers, and you could hear them coming.

After a while, I heard my wife begin to cry quietly. Little by little, her crying increased in intensity until she was wracked with sobs. "Is this what you meant when you told me about the will of the Lord for us?" she sobbed. "I came from a poor home, but I have never ever slept on a newspaper before. I am

Contentment

going home tomorrow to my Daddy." She was really feeling sorry for herself.

I thought to myself, "It will be hard for her to go home tomorrow — since we came on a one-way ticket." But her distress was catching, and very soon I began feeling sorry for us too. I didn't tell her how I was feeling, because I knew that it would only make her feel worse. But she continued crying for a long time.

I began to pray, and suddenly, God spoke to me. He said:

If you will be content, if you will be happy with your circumstances and will serve Me in the midst of your difficulty, I will prosper you and bless you as you have never dreamed of being blessed. But if you insist on complaining and murmuring and having a sour spirit, you will become poor, as poor as a rat that has no hole in which to hide.

That hit me like a bolt of lightening, and I started praising God. I grabbed my wife and I said, "Honey, the Lord just spoke to me."

"What?" she said gruffly, "Are we going to go home tomorrow?"

"No," I said. "The Lord showed me that if we will be content, if we will be satisfied, if we will rejoice in every state we find ourselves in, and will serve Him faithfully in the midst of our difficulty, He will open the windows of Heaven and bless us."

I faced her and said, "Let's praise the Lord together."

She said, "You praise the Lord yourself. I can't do it right now."

She was sitting on the floor, using a towel as a fan to keep the mosquitoes off the baby.

I began to worship the Lord, thanking Him for His goodness, remembering Calvary, remembering the pit from which I was dug.

I realized what a privilege it was to serve God — in any circumstances. After a while, the glory of the Lord came down in that place. I grabbed my wife and held her closely to me, and we rejoiced together and praised God in the Spirit. It was so glorious I didn't want it to end.

The next morning we woke up content. God had completely changed our attitude. Our hearts were rejoicing. We had committed everything to Him. Whether we lived or died, we were the Lord's, and we were at peace with our situation. There was no recourse, and there would be no surrender. We had

Contentment

to go forward. But God was on our side, so how could we lose?

That very day God began to move on our behalf. I met a pastor while I was out distributing tracts. He invited us to visit his church. Later, through a series of unusual miracles, God moved on members of his church to bring us food, and blankets, and towels, and appliances — and everything else we needed. We had to distribute the weight of our blessings around the house at various points so the house wouldn't collapse.

Two weeks later, an American man invited us to house-sit for him while he was on vacation in the States. He loaded the house down with food and left word in the grocery store to give us whatever was lacking. We stayed there for a month. Then the Lord opened the door to another house. The owner of the first house was arriving that day, and the other family was leaving the same day. We just moved our things over to the other house.

When our three weeks were up, my wife asked me, "Where do we go now?" I knew that if we didn't grumble the Lord would provide.

I was conducting Bible studies in the base, preaching in the local jail, and teaching Sunday school in the church. Now, the church decided to hire me full-time as a janitor and to provide us an apartment.

Six months later, the pastor went back to the States, and we became the new pastors of the church. As pastors, we moved to the lovely furnished parsonage. It was air-conditioned (no small thing in a tropical climate), it had a washer, dryer, and floor polisher. It was complete. My wife started to cry as she thanked the Lord for showing us the secret of prosperity, "Lord, we don't deserve all of this, but we thank You."

Since that time, God has continued to bless our family more and more. We have learned that contentment is powerful, and we will never be caught in the trap of grumbling and complaining again.

If you will be content in your marriage, your marriage will take on a new excitement that you never imagined, and you will be blessed of God.

Many children and young people are not content with their home situation. For their sake, I want to summarize the testimony of a young American who told me his story. I was so impressed with what he told me that I have repeated it in every marriage and family seminar I have conducted. Let it serve as a lesson for those children and young people who have Christian parents, but are not happy with the way things go at home.

Contentment

I grew up in a very poor family. Our parents raised us on food stamps, because our father had a limited education, was disabled, and could not work. There were many of us children, and my mother had a hard time taking care of us.

It always embarrassed me to go to the store with my mother. I was afraid that one of my classmates or friends would see her paying the cashier with the food stamps.

I graduated from high school with only two pairs of trousers and a single pair of shoes to my name. When we went to church, we were unable to put even a nickel into the offering. We were totally deprived of earthly possessions.

All of us children began to work at a very young age and to try to continue our education.

He stood tall and straight and looked directly into my eyes. Then, with a broad smile on his face and pride evident upon his countenance (but with tears streaming from his eyes), he continued:

The only thing my parents gave us was a love for God. They taught us how to pray and exercise our faith. Never did we hear our parents argue because there was nothing in the house to eat. We did hear

> *them weep and cry out to God. At some of these times, a knock would come at the door and someone would be standing there with something they had been led to bring for us to eat. I know that this is a heritage the world could never have given us.*

His father had only gone to the fourth grade, and his mother had not finished high school, but he was very proud of them:

> *There is something our parents gave us that I am very proud of. It compensated for the lack of material things. The riches that Mom and Dad gave us is our personal experience with God.*

This part of the story was particularly interesting to me:

> *We had a neighbor who was very wealthy. The son was cruel and would torment us. They had a beautiful house, and ours was of the lowest quality. They had a beautiful car, and we had none. He was always well-dressed and had money in his pocket. We walked to school and back, while he rode. He finished high school and went on to college, but he didn't do well in life and is now in jail, for hav-*

Contentment

ing been involved in a loan company fraud case.

I think he started going bad when his father, a wealthy businessman, would go out of town on business, and, while he was gone, another man would visit the mother. Before long, the couple was divorced. The mother remarried and divorced two more times.

Our parents, on the other hand, demonstrated to us unity, harmony and a good relationship in the midst of all their troubles. They stuck together through thick and thin. Nothing was more important to them than the family.

They are gone now, but the five of us children who are still living get together once a year to rejoice together over our great inheritance.

Contentment is a powerful force. Put it to work in your own life, and you will be blessed and on your way toward finding God's order for your family. ➔

Chapter 9

Consistency

Know ye not that they which run in a race run all, but one receiveth the prize? So run, that ye may obtain. And every man that striveth for the mastery is temperate in all things. Now they do it to obtain a corruptible crown; but we an incorruptible. I therefore so run, not as uncertainly; so fight I, not as one that beateth the air:
1 Corinthians 9:24-26

Wherefore seeing we also are compassed about with so great a cloud of witnesses, let us lay aside every weight, and the sin which doth so easily beset us, and let us run with patience the race that is set before us, Hebrews 12:1

Not everyone who begins a race wins a prize. Those who finish the race win. It is the same with married life and the family. Commitment to the marriage and to the family brings contentment; and

Consistency

contentment brings consistency, a willingness to *"run with patience"* until the goal is reached.

We might call this consistency a "sticktuitiveness." If the bond of marriage is well glued, it won't easily come unstuck.

It reminds me of the tiny house lizards we have in the tropics. They are harmless and actually beneficial, because they dart about eating insects. The amazing thing about them is that they can walk upside down on the ceiling. Something about their feet helps them cling to the ceiling in that precarious position and not fall.

When we take the wedding vows, we are committing ourselves to consistency. We say:

For better or for worse,
For richer or for poorer,
In sickness and in health,
Until death do us part.

We are promising God and our mate that we will stick with our commitment in sunshine and in rain, when things are going well and when things are not going so well, when we feel like it and when we don't feel like it any more. We are in a race, reaching for the goal, striving ever upward. There is no giving up.

Founded On the Rock

Our young people who are getting married these days have no consistency. They have no "sticktuitiveness." When the first problem arises, they are ready to pack it in. When the first disagreement comes, they are ready to abandon the ship. No wonder they don't last long! How could they?

No marriage is free of problems. No home is free of disagreement. No relationship is free of friction. But you can't give up with the first little windstorm that comes along. You have to get serious and commit to this thing for the long haul. This is a lifetime commitment, so stick with it, and you will have victory.

Be consistent. Keep on keeping on. Do not be blown about by every slight wind. Do not be moved by the circumstances of life. If you are shaken by little things, what will you do when the really big problems of life arise?

And they will come. There are many giants that we must face in life. Sometimes they are so big that we feel like grasshoppers in their sight. But we cannot give up. We must face every giant and win; and we can win because the Lord makes us strong in our weakness.

You may face the giant of financial problems. Most of us do at some point in our married life.

Consistency

You may face the giant of in-law interference in your marriage. It is very common — all over the world. You may face the giant of misunderstanding with your mate or with your children. If so, look to God, and begin to rejoice in His strength. Thank God that you are a grasshopper. The giants will have trouble finding you among the tall grass.

Giants cannot easily step on us and squash us because they are so big we can see them coming. Praise God!

You may be thinking, *The giants of my marriage are just too big. What can I do? It is beyond my ability to deal with them. I am not up to the challenge.*

Rejoice, and be happy. It is hard to miss such a big target. Rejoice, and be happy. God is on our side.

When you look at the difficulty, when you look at the varied personalities, the rough character of your husband or wife, the likes and the dislikes of each one of you, they seem insurmountable. You pray, "God in Heaven, will this marriage work?"

Grumblers and complainers would give up quickly, saying "This thing is too big for me to face. We might as well give up and get a divorce."

But the spirit of commitment inside of you will insist, "NO WAY! You can defeat this giant with your eyes closed. He is too big to miss." Believe it and act upon it.

With one stone, you can topple the giant that threatens to destroy you and your marriage, and you and your spouse will live happily the rest of your lives together, committed to one another, content with one another, and consistently loving one another to the glory of God.

The consistency of commitment and contentment brings a flow of the rivers of peace, rivers of harmony, and rivers of love. You and your spouse can make beautiful music together.

In order to be consistent in your marriage and in your family life, you must recognize and overcome the many outside influences bent on your destruction. I want to name a few of the most powerful and destructive ones:

Meddling In-Laws

In-laws often don't use wisdom with their newly married children. It is hard for them to realize that their "baby" has grown up and married and now has a life of his or her own. They often meddle in your affairs. You must learn to deal with this in a loving but firm way.

If you are a father-in law or a mother-in-law, don't be caught in this trap. Let your married children

Consistency

alone to work out their own problems, and don't say anything unless you are asked. You have no right to make decisions for your married children now. You can make suggestions, but it is up to them to receive or reject your suggestions. Once your children are grown and married, they must make their own decisions in life. You cannot continue to make decisions for them.

THE TEMPTATION TO CONFORM TO THE WORLD'S STANDARD

We are bombarded day and night, through television and radio, through print media, and through the lives others are living around us, to conform to the world's standard. The Scriptures say:

For whom he did foreknow, he also did predestinate to be conformed to the image of his Son, that he might be the firstborn among many brethren.
Romans 8:29

And be not conformed to this world: but be ye transformed by the renewing of your mind, that ye may prove what is that good, and acceptable, and perfect, will of God. Romans 12:2

We are saved and transformed by grace so that we can conform to the image of God's only begotten Son. Do not allow the worldly spirit to creep in and take control of your desire.

Worldliness is coming into the Church and, consequently, the divorce rate among Christians is approaching the rate of divorce for the public at large! We cannot be like this world. And if we are, we are no longer like Christ and cease to be true Christians.

Being a believer in name only will not get you to Heaven, and accepting the worldly attitudes and habits of nominal Christians will do your marriage and your home irreparable damage.

In that same vein, we have the influence we have come to call:

PEER PRESSURE

"Everybody is doing it."

"We are the abnormal ones. We are the only ones who are not doing it."

Well, thank God that we know better. Thank God that we know the difference between right and wrong. Thank God that we can be different from the world.

Consistency

Don't be pressured by your friends. Don't be influenced by your office mates. Only be influenced by the principles of God's Word. Only be governed and influenced by His standard of excellence.

Peer pressure is destroying thousands of our young people, and if you are not careful, peer pressure will attack every member of your household.

Too Much Television

Everyone is in agreement: television is one of the most powerful influences in our twentieth century society, and most everyone agrees that it does far more harm than it does good. Thank God for the educational and informative benefits of television. But don't accept everything put forth for the public on television. Many of its programs are very dangerous to your spiritual well-being.

Be careful what you are watching. Choose your programs carefully. If a program is not edifying, if it is not honest, if it is not true, if it is not godly, if it is not pure, if there is no virtue in it, and there is no praise in it, you have no business watching it. For these are the tests of validity and value the Scriptures place on every type of media:

Finally, brethren, whatsoever things are true, whatsoever things are honest, whatsoever things are just, whatsoever things are pure, whatsoever things are lovely, whatsoever things are of good report; if there be any virtue, and if there be any praise, think on these things. Philippians 4:8

According to recent statistics, most of the crime committed in the United States is inspired, in whole or in part, by what children see on television. When you turn on your television, you see rape, murder, wife beating, child abuse, disrespect for parents — and much more. Everything you see has an influence on your mind and on your soul. It can get hold of you and start controlling your thinking.

Husbands and wives are guilty of sitting up together to see the late-late movie until the wee hours of the morning on Saturday night. Then they have a hard time getting up for church. Soap operas and other similar programs have done irreparable damage to our present generation.

It is from such programs that many get ideas about cheating on their spouses, swapping spouses, or defrauding a friend. We are so bombarded with this filth weekly that, little by little, the devil is using

Consistency

it to press us into the world's mold, and to make us conform to the standard of the world.

The tragedy is that this filth is so accepted by society at large. The fact is that if you have been married for forty years and still have the same husband or wife, society considers you to be abnormal. More normally, you change your spouse about every few years. That's the kind of society in which we find ourselves living.

That outside influence is coming more and more into Christian circles. Guard your city well. Don't allow the enemy to take what is yours.

If you are to have consistency in the marriage and in the home, you must also avoid many of the failures that have been common among Christian families. Some of them are:

SPIRITUAL INCONSISTENCY IN THE HOME

By that, I mean that parents say one thing and do another thing. They live a hypocritical life, having the appearance of holiness before the members of their church, but looking very much like any other sinner in their dealings with their family. Children especially are adversely affected by this. They hate a phony.

Founded On the Rock

Failure to Make God the Lord Over Your Marriage and Over Your Family

We have the habit of praying to God for the prosperity of the home, but we are not in the habit of asking God to govern us, to be Lord and Master over us. By the way we live, we are actually saying, "Lord, it's okay for You to bless us, but You have no right to rule over us."

The success of your marriage, the blessing and prosperity of your home depends on your making Jesus Lord of every facet of your personal life. He must be the center of every activity, the center of all planning, the center of your thinking and your acting, the focal point, the central figure of everything, so that everything you do, as a couple and as a family, you do to the glory of God.

If your commitment to Jesus is shallow, your commitment to the marriage will be even more shallow. When your commitment to Christ is deep, your relationship with your spouse will deepen also. Make Him Lord of your personal life, Lord of your marriage, and Lord of your home.

Consistency

FAILURE TO APPLY THE WORD OF GOD AS THE GUIDING PRINCIPLE THAT GOVERNS YOUR LIVES

We have the attitude that it is our right to demand from God all the promises and the blessings, without recognizing His rights over us. We do have the right to demand what God has promised us. We are His children, and God is not a liar. He is a faithful, covenant-keeping God. What He has promised, He will do. It is not wrong to know our rights and to claim them. Most of us are quick to learn this lesson.

But the truth is that God has more rights over us than we have from Him. He is Lord, He is Master, and, as Lord and Master of our lives, His rights are uppermost. We are not our own. We are bought with a price. We are purchased by His own blood. It is no longer I that live, but Christ that lives in me.

> *I am crucified with Christ: nevertheless I live; yet not I, but Christ liveth in me: and the life which I now live in the flesh I live by the faith of the Son of God, who loved me, and gave himself for me.*
> Galatians 2:20

We are already dead. We have been crucified with Christ and have been resurrected to walk in the newness of life. We need to give up all rights and recognize that He has all rights over us.

When we apply that knowledge to the marriage and to the family, the blessing of God will come without measure. Harmony and peace and unity will be there, because the enemy has no power to overcome us — when we are submitted to God's will.

We must teach our children that the Bible is the final authority when it comes to lifestyle. We have already covered this point when talking about the influence the world is having over our Christian youth. But it is so important that we need to emphasize it. Teach your young people that the Bible is not out-of-date, as they are being told in school. Show them historically that those who have obeyed the Bible have also prospered, and those who have not obeyed the Bible have suffered the consequences.

Failure to Recognize the Need to Be Involved in Church Activities

Attending church services on Sunday is not enough. The church must become an integral part of our everyday existence. When a family is actively engaged in the programs of the church, it is rare that their children depart from God. Don't just take

Consistency

your family to church. Teach them to be involved in the activities of the church. Find a church that has activities for all ages, and get your children involved in those activities.

Give your family the high sense of value for the importance of the church in their lives. Never let your children feel that it's "a drag" to go to church. David said:

> *I was glad when they said unto me, Let us go into the house of the LORD.* Psalm 122:1

Church attendance is not only good when it is convenient. It is good whether it is convenient or not. Church attendance is good not just when we feel up to it. If is also good when we don't feel up to it. We must be faithful in this area. It is an integral part of our growing-up process.

Never send your children to Sunday school and stay home yourself. That teaches them the wrong attitude. Take them to Sunday school. And they are never too young. Get them into the Sunday school habit early.

Most churches have a very diminished attendance on Sunday evening, and they feel fortunate if even ten percent of the members show up for a mid-week service. Don't you be one of those no-shows. And don't arrive when the service is half over. Be on time.

Don't just get involved in attendance. Learn to support the church with your tithes and offerings. You may think that your church doesn't need your money and that you can send your tithes somewhere else, but that is not biblical. Pay your tithes where they belong. If you do it, God will bless you. He has irrevocably ordered it to be so.

Find some work that needs to be done in the church. Don't wait to be asked. Volunteer your time and talents, so that your children will learn the joys of serving God.

An Unforgiving Spirit

Nothing can destroy a marriage or a home as fast as an unforgiving spirit, and it never fails. It will destroy you — if you don't get rid of it.

You cannot afford to hold any grudges or resentment against your spouse or your children. If they made a mistake, forgive them and forget. Then, don't ever mention it again. Don't keep throwing it up to them.

Jesus linked our willingness to forgive others to His ability to forgive us of our own failures:

Consistency

For if ye forgive men their trespasses, your heavenly Father will also forgive you: But if ye forgive not men their trespasses, neither will your Father forgive your trespasses.   Matthew 6:14-15

And his lord was wroth, and delivered him to the tormentors, till he should pay all that was due unto him. So likewise shall my heavenly Father do also unto you, if ye from your hearts forgive not every one his brother their trespasses.

Matthew 18:34-35

And when ye stand praying, forgive, if ye have ought against any: that your Father also which is in heaven may forgive you your trespasses. But if ye do not forgive, neither will your Father which is in heaven forgive your trespasses.

Mark 11:25-26

Judge not, and ye shall not be judged: condemn not, and ye shall not be condemned: forgive, and ye shall be forgiven: Luke 6:37

Your willingness to forgive is also linked, in scripture, to the blessing you will receive in the communion service (see 1 Corinthians 11:29) and the reward you will have for your financial giving (see Matthew 5:23-24).

As we have seen, unresolved friction in the marriage can hinder your prayers.

> *Likewise, ye husbands, dwell with them according to knowledge, giving honour unto the wife, as unto the weaker vessel, and as being heirs together of the grace of life; that your prayers be not hindered.*
> 1 Peter 3:7

Christ has forgiven you, and He now expects you to forgive others. If you do not, it is a symbol of your lack of appreciation for what He has done for you.

> *Forbearing one another, and forgiving one another, if any man have a quarrel against any: even as Christ forgave you, so also do ye.* Colossians 3:13

You cannot afford to take this teaching lightly. Learn to forgive. You can do it, and you must.

THE LACK OF CHRISTIAN DISCIPLINE

We all fall short in this category. Most of us do not have enough systematic Bible reading or enough

Consistency

systematic devotional time. Our excuse is always that there is no time. But, when a person is disciplined, there is always enough time for important things. Lack of discipline wastes a lot of time and a lot of energy.

Discipline yourself. If you know you need to get up at 5:00 a.m. to spend time with the Lord before you go to work, resist the temptation to sit up watching that late-night movie. Stop gossiping on the telephone and go to bed early so that you can get up on time. Because we are not disciplined in this regard, we have time to listen to all the garbage of the world and no time for God. And if parents are lacking in this regard, what can we expect of our children?

We seem to have plenty of time to sit down with friends and laugh. We seem to have plenty of time for the nonsense and foolish things of the world. Why is it that we have so little time to pray? Let us all work on living more disciplined lives.

THE LACK OF A SPIRITUAL ATMOSPHERE IN THE HOME

I asked a man with whom I was counseling, "Why is it that you don't go home on time?"

He replied, "My work is a Hell. By the time I finish eight hours, I am burned out. I don't want to go home, because it is another Hell." Many children feel the same way.

Parents, it is your responsibility to create a spiritual atmosphere in your home so that your children will love to run home to find solitude. Make home a haven for your children. Then, they will want to come home instead of going to places they have no business going.

Many of those who have run away from home have done so because Mom and Dad are like two cats, fighting all the time. Create an atmosphere that is wholesome, godly, righteous and with a spiritual tone, and they will not run away.

You can create such an atmosphere only when you have become spiritual and in tune with the Lord yourself. It doesn't just happen.

Nothing could be more important for the future well-being of your family. Even if you have tiny children, the atmosphere in which they grow is important.

When God entrusts to us a newborn baby, it is our responsibility to provide for that child an atmosphere conducive to growth. All life in fact, needs the proper atmosphere in which to grow. When we raise plants, we must understand if they are indoor plants or outdoor plants. If you put an indoor plant

Consistency

outside, it will die because it lacks the atmosphere conducive for its growth. If you put an outdoor plant inside, sooner or later it will die. Parents, it is your responsibility, as members of the Body of Christ, and as the leadership of your household, to create a proper spiritual atmosphere in your home.

An old saying goes: **"There's no place like home."** That can be true. There is no place like a peaceful home. There is nothing like a home filled with Christian music, a home filled with the prayers of Mom and Dad. Maybe you heard you mother singing while she was cooking or washing, and you never forgot it. It is a picture forever imposed on the lens of your soul.

But who likes to go home when you know that upon opening the door you will hear arguments and curses? When children miss Heaven, usually it is the parents who are to blame. That is a strong statement, but it is the truth.

Why are there so many wayward children? Because they cannot stand being at home. Why? Because their home is not a happy place. Their home is a battlefield.

Prayer, Bible reading, meditation and exhortation will create an atmosphere conducive to spiritual growth and maturity for every member of the family. If we will create such an atmosphere, beloved, we will save ourselves a lot of heartache and a lot of wasted energy.

It can be a beautiful thing when Mom and Dad have a problem, if, instead of hearing or seeing them fighting, the children hear them praying together and crying out to the Lord. That is a healthy atmosphere in which children learn what to do when they have problems of their own. They will also cry to God instead of fighting with one another.

It is a blessing for children to grow up in an atmosphere of financial need, if, when things are tight, they hear their parents say to them, "Son [or daughter], our God will provide." And rather than blaming each other and fighting with each other or running around borrowing from here and from there, they pray together and trust the Lord Jehovah Jireh, and God provides. When those children grow up, they will have faith built into their thinking, and what they saw their parents do they will also do. Now is the time to get faith into you children, to teach them to trust, to have confidence in God.

It is our responsibility to create that wholesome, godly, righteous, spiritual atmosphere, an atmosphere with a tone of love to God and a respect for each other, and where Jesus is recognized as Lord

Consistency

and Master of every activity in the house and in the life of every member of the family. Nothing could be better preparation for your child's future.

Mom and Dad, your children will copy whatever you do. They will follow your lead. You are the potter, and they are the clay. You are molding lives. Take care how you treat this great responsibility.

The creation of the wholesome atmosphere in which you and your children can thrive is not the responsibility of the husband alone and not the responsibility of the wife alone. It is your mutual responsibility to make it happen. Work at it together. Help each other.

Wife, if you get home first, think of what you can do to refresh you husband when he comes home tired from work.

Husband, think of what you can do to prepare for the arrival of your wife, something to freshen the atmosphere and cause her to feel better once she gets home.

Some of the things that disturb the peace of the home are obvious. For instance, turn off the rock and roll. If the children must hear it, send them somewhere else. Put on some soft, gentle and relaxing music. If the sink is full of dirty dishes, wash them before your wife gets home. Little things like this make a big difference.

Do the same type of things for the children. Most of all, make them feel at home so that they won't be tempted to go to the streets.

By analyzing the outside influences that attempt to hinder your marriage and your home, and by looking at some of the more common failures in Christian homes, I trust that you will build a greater consistency in your marriage and in your home, until nothing will be able to do you harm. Take these important steps toward finding God's order for your family. →

Part IV

Special Biblical Advice

Chapter 10

Advice to Singles

Be ye not unequally yoked together with unbelievers: for what fellowship hath righteousness with unrighteousness? and what communion hath light with darkness? And what concord hath Christ with Belial? or what part hath he that believeth with an infidel? And what agreement hath the temple of God with idols? for ye are the temple of the living God; as God hath said, I will dwell in them, and walk in them; and I will be their God, and they shall be my people. Wherefore come out from among them, and be ye separate, saith the Lord, and touch not the unclean thing; and I will receive you. And will be a Father unto you, and ye shall be my sons and daughters, saith the Lord Almighty.

Having therefore these promises, dearly beloved, let us cleanse ourselves from all filthiness of the flesh and spirit, perfecting holiness in the fear of God.   2 Corinthians 6:14-7:1

When the Bible instructs young people not to marry unbelievers, it does not do so with the aim of robbing them of their fun in life. God knows the future. He knows that without Him, there is no lasting happiness. Every young person would like to have a happy marriage, but what they don't understand is that only God can grant us that dream.

I want to join my voice to that of the Apostle Paul in saying: do not marry someone who is not in the Kingdom of God. If you do, you are only asking for trouble. If you want your home to prosper, if you want to have peace of mind, follow the instructions given by God to Paul for the people of his day.

"But, Pastor," the young ladies say, "I have been bringing him to church."

Well, church is not enough. He has to get into the Kingdom of God.

"But he came to the altar and cried."

Yes, a lot of people cry in the altar; but some of those tears are not genuine. They are what we commonly call "crocodile tears." Young men can put on a very good show when they are trying to win the hearts of some Christian young lady.

"Oh, pastor, he was baptized in water. He is a Christian."

Advice to Singles

Oh, is he really? Probably the only difference in him was that he went in dry and came out wet.

As you can see, I am very skeptical when it comes to the courting practices of unbelievers. I have reason to be. This is serious business. When you decide to marry, it is for life. It is forever. You cannot return or exchange what you bought in the department store of life. When you marry, you enter into a binding agreement. It is lasting. So, find someone who is a God-fearing women, a God-fearing man, a person who has a heart after God, a person who is spiritually awakened to the things of God. Find somebody who has a definite, solid, firm relationship with God. And I guarantee you that you will have a happy married life.

Young people come to me and say, "I led him to the Lord. He is now a Christian."

A lot of people can parrot what they hear others saying, without ever having an experience of their own. That doesn't mean they are saved. Be careful. That is all I ask.

If I were a young person who had never been married before, I would be very afraid to commit my life to someone that did not know the Lord. Even though we Christians know the Lord, we are often hard on each other. We lack patience with one another. How much more someone who doesn't know the Lord, a person who is controlled by the god of this world, who is ignorant of righteousness and the principles of the Kingdom of God!

Young people, listen to me, it would be better for you to put a big millstone around your neck and throw yourself into the sea than to marry such a person. Marrying an unsaved person is tantamount to committing suicide. Avoid all that deep sorrow by having patience now and making a wise decision regarding your future mate.

When I perform a wedding, at the end of the vow taking, I usually say to the bride and groom: "Now, your shopping days are over. All the department stores of life are closed. No exchange. No return. Take it home and enjoy it. If you don't enjoy it, work at it until you do enjoy it. Stick to it because there is no retreat and no surrender. From here on out, it is always *advance* and *forward*."

This is serious business, and you cannot afford to make a mistake.

"But, Pastor, I am really in love with him."

I beg your pardon. Usually what we call *love* is not love at all. It is LUST and there is a BIG difference. We use that word LOVE so much. "I love ... , I love ... ." But usually it is LUST, GREED, and the WORK OF THE FLESH.

Advice to Singles

I tried to counsel a young lady in San Francisco. She was twenty-three and had been itching to get out of the house. Her mother told her that she could only leave home when she got married, so she began praying that the Lord would send her a young man.

The problem was that all the young men who had been knocking at the door of her heart were unbelievers. Then, along came a young, handsome bachelor. He had a beautiful dimple in his chin. When he smiled, the young girls were electrified.

He applied for a job in the company where she worked and was hired. Before long, all the young ladies had their eyes on him. They even started making bets as to who would be the first one to be asked for a date.

This girl was the one he asked first.

She could hardly believe her good luck. "Me?"

"Yes."

She accepted, and the young man took her to a disco. Since she had grown up in church, she didn't know how to dance, but he told her that he would teach her. As they went to the middle of the floor, her heart was beating fast. He put his arms around her, and they began dancing together. *I have a great catch here,* she thought.

But when the mother knew that the relationship was getting serious, she did not agree. "This must stop," she said. "This man is not a Christian."

"But, Mama, he is coming to church on Sunday," the girl protested.

"Well, he must get saved before you spend any more time with him."

"Mama, I will introduce him to Pastor Ray on Sunday. I know he will be saved."

She brought him to my office. I sat him down across the desk from me and talked to him about the Lord. To everything I said, he grunted, "Uh huh!"

Be careful! Those who always agree may be dangerous, wanting something else, and they will agree to almost anything to get what they want.

I sensed that the boy was not sincere and told this girl, "You are asking for trouble."

"But, Pastor Llarena, how can you say that? I am twenty-three years old already. This is the only prospect I have. No one else has even looked at me. I haven't had a date with another man." And I could see that she had made up her mind and that there was no use in my trying to convince her otherwise. There was nothing that I could do. There was nothing that her parents could do. Even the Holy Ghost was powerless to stop her from

Advice to Singles

proceeding with her plans. She was "in love." So, she got married.

In only three months she was back in my office with her mother by her side. Her eye was black and blue, and there was a cut over it. "I should have listened to you," she bewailed, but it was too late. I have never forgotten the sadness in her eyes. It is better to use a little prevention in regard to an unhappy marriage than to later have to apply a cure. As the old saying goes: *An ounce of prevention is worth more than a pound of cure.*

Many believers marry in this way, out of excitement, and wake up to find themselves joined to an unbeliever. When they realize what has happened, they want to back out and say they have made a mistake. "Can my wedding be annulled?" they ask.

I tell them it is too late for that. If they have gotten themselves into a mess, they will just have to stay there and work to resolve the problems. Running away doesn't resolve anything. Two wrongs don't make a right.

"But Pastor," they complain, "the furnace is getting hotter."

"Then you are going to get fried," I tell them. "Grin and bear it. This was your foolish choice. You asked for it. Now, learn your lesson well. And pray for the rapture to take place soon so that you escape your commitment. There is no other solution."

"One mistake cannot be corrected by making another mistake. If you made a mistake, repent, and seek God so that your spouse will come to know Him and have everlasting life. Abandoning the home will not solve anything. It will only complicate your problem and add more sorrow and remorse to your life."

Divorce must be the most extreme solution to marital conflict. It is never God's perfect solution to the problem. Before any person starts thinking about divorce, they must try everything they can try to mend the marriage, to patch things up, to work out the differences, and restore the marriage. It is possible, with the Lord's help, to restore a weakened building to the place that it is better than it ever was.

Young Christian ladies seem to be more susceptible to nonbelieving men. Young ladies, listen to me, when a young man comes to court you and he is not a believer, ninety percent of the time he is not interested in you as a person. He only wants to take advantage of you. When you first meet, he is very polite. He just holds your hand. On the second date, he is already caressing your shoulders and hugging you. On the third date, he is already saying, "If you

Advice to Singles

really love me, prove it to me. How can I know that you really love me if you won't give me what I want NOW?"

You may say, "Let's wait until we get married."

But he will reply, "What is the difference? Let's try it now. Then we will know."

That type of man is not worthy of your hand in marriage. Drop him like a hot potato, and find the man of integrity that God has prepared for you.

I know what I am talking about. I am over fifty years old and have worked with young people for many years. I have counseled a lot of young ladies. I have had to deal with those who are going through the remorse of an abortion, those who are suffering from the shame of their acts, and those who are suddenly mothers when they are still teenagers and have hardly finished their childhood.

I adjure you by the living God, protect your virginity until you meet that perfect man or woman that God has prepared for you.

Just last year a man came into my office for counseling. He said, "Pastor, I am already forty years old, and I'm still a virgin." He said it as if it were some tragedy and something to be sad about.

I jumped up and said, "Praise God! That's wonderful! I meet so many who have not protected themselves. I am glad to meet someone who has."

Even now, as I write this revision of the original text, I am counseling with a couple who plan to marry. Both of them are virgins. Thank God for Christian young people who keep themselves holy. Do it for the Lord and for your future mate. God has set aside the perfect mate for you. Wait patiently for him or her.

"How long will it take before he comes, Pastor?"

It's not how long, but how patiently will you wait for God's perfect mate? Most of our sorrow, most of our pain, most of our heartache we create for ourselves and bring upon ourselves because of impatience. When all your classmates are already married and you are the only one left single, everyone is asking, "What's wrong with you? Why are you not yet married?" If you are a virgin, they think there must be something wrong with you. When it comes time for your class reunion, everyone is asking you if you are gay; and, if not, why are you not yet married?

Many people are moved by this pressure to marry — by hook or by crook. But don't be moved by what people say. Not every person who declines to get married is gay or lesbian. I have declined to remarry since my wife died, and that doesn't make me less of

Advice to Singles

a man. Marriage doesn't prove anything. It doesn't make you a real man or a real women. Married or unmarried, you must prove yourself faithful in the eyes of God.

Just being a husband or a wife does not make you something more or less in this world. Be content with your state. That is God's best for your life. Accept that fact and be content with it.

When you accept your status, married or single, as from God, and you strive to be the best Christian you can be in your circumstances, you bless the heart of God. Men who are married should strive to be the best husband and the best father they can be. Women who are married should strive to be the best wife and the best mother they can be.

Singles must be the best singles they can be. Keep yourself holy before God. Be content with your status. As Paul taught the Corinthians:

> *Art thou bound unto a wife? seek not to be loosed.*
> *Art thou loosed from a wife? seek not a wife.*
> 1 Corinthians 7:27

This advice, inspired by God Himself, was to not seek to be single and to not seek to be married. That is the best advice. Wait for God's perfect timing to get married, and don't marry for any other reason.

Until you do get married, be careful how you touch each other. Even if you are already engaged, be careful. The devil can use your touching to destroy your testimony.

I am of the opinion that it is not proper for young people to begin kissing each other on their first, second and third dates. That has nothing to do with being a Filipino or being an American. It is just not right, and it leads to tragedy.

Young people go to the pizza shop to share a pizza and get acquainted, and they are already kissing each other in the car. Usually, they know nothing about each other, what they might or might not feel for each other, or what, if any, future they might have together. That is very dangerous. It is playing with fire, and it is not wise. When two lips touch, sparks fly and fire begins to smolder. Don't play with fire.

Christian men, when you are courting a girl, you must treat her with a Christian attitude and with Christian behavior, protecting her and preserving her for the day you may say, "I DO."

And the same is true for the girls. Some women these days are more aggressive than the men. Do

Advice to Singles

not be carried away with your emotions and do things for which you will later be very sorry. If you feel something bubbling up inside, that may or may not be love. That may or may not be from God. Be careful! Your emotions can lead you into tragedy.

Most young ladies do not intend to get pregnant before marriage, but because they are not careful when touching each other, they get carried away with the emotion of the moment and have to pay the rest of their lives.

There are many areas of the body where you have no right to be touching each other before marriage. If you do it, you are just asking for trouble. You cannot play with fire without getting burned, and burns leave scars. No matter how wonderfully the skin heals, there are always scars that remain.

There must be boundaries and limitations. You can be intimately acquainted with each other without any physical contact whatsoever. You can be expressive without going too far. It is worth it to arrive at the wedding day without the scars of foolish mistakes.

Many young people are forced to marry before the proper time. If a man can hardly support himself, how can he support a family? But when they have foolishly been carried away with their emotions, they are forced to play hide and seek, expressing their emotions for one another in stolen moments of secrecy. This is not a rewarding relationship. They are groping on the back seat of a car in a dark park or some other semiprivate place. Then, when the girl becomes pregnant, they are forced to get married. And, perhaps because one or both of them has not finished their studies, or because the man has not found a job yet, they are forced to live a less-than-rewarding existence. Not a very good backdrop for their love!

It may indeed be the will of God for these two to marry, but they have not been willing to wait for the correct timing. Now, because they will undoubtedly suffer many hardships, through financial insecurity, they will eventually begin to take out their frustrations on each other and to fight with each other. Their moments of stolen passion will ruin their life of love together and perhaps leave them both destroyed.

In moments of anger, she might say, "If you had only been willing to leave me alone and not insist on proving my love to you, we would not have ended up like this."

Advice to Singles

The husband might say, "I remember that you were enjoying yourself and were even asking for it. So, what are you complaining about?"

When this happens, that couple is in serious trouble, for this argument will deteriorate into a battle, and the battle into a war that can only end with both sides losing.

So when you relate to each other, maintain a Christian testimony, that everything you do, whatever it may be, you do to the glory of God.

There is another area in which I feel compelled to admonish singles:

What you are is God's gift to you. Why try to change that? Many men want to change their appearance. They are wearing makeup and long fingernails and wearing dresses. When they go out, they walk like ladies. But why do you want to be something different than God made you? He knows best. Trust Him, and don't try to be different.

Many ladies are trying to be macho men. They cut their hair short and wear T-shirts and jeans. But they are mistaken. If God made you a woman, don't try to change that fact. What you are is your gift from God. Be satisfied as God made you. Don't try to change yourself. What you become is your gift to God.

Founded On the Rock

If you, as a single person, are living in disobedience to the Word of God, you cannot expect Him to bless you. And what do you hope to gain? Live for God, and you will have His best.

Even as singles, you have an important role to play in finding God's order for your life. →

Chapter 11

Advice to Ministers

A bishop then must be blameless, the husband of one wife, vigilant, sober, of good behaviour, given to hospitality, apt to teach; Not given to wine, no striker, not greedy of filthy lucre; but patient, not a brawler, not covetous; One that ruleth well his own house, having his children in subjection with all gravity; (For if a man know not how to rule his own house, how shall he take care of the church of God?) Not a novice, lest being lifted up with pride he fall into the condemnation of the devil. Moreover he must have a good report of them which are without; lest he fall into reproach and the snare of the devil.

Likewise must the deacons be grave, not double-tongued, not given to much wine, not greedy of filthy lucre; Holding the mystery of the faith in a pure conscience. And let these also first be proved; then let them use the office of a deacon, being found blameless. Even so must their wives be grave, not slanderers, sober, faithful in all things. Let the deacons be the husbands of one wife, ruling their children and their own houses well. For they that have used the office of a deacon well purchase to themselves a good degree, and great boldness in the faith which is in Christ Jesus.

1 Timothy 3:2-13

There is always a danger, for those who are in Christian ministry, to confuse the priorities of the family and the priorities of the ministry. You may not agree with me on this point, but I am convinced that the reason the children of church workers are often wayward and find themselves in the cesspool of the world is that they are always put last in the list of priorities. I have come to that conclusion through years of counseling with Christian leaders, including deacons, women's leaders, Sunday school teachers, and even pastors.

We can all agree that our number one ministry is to God Himself, but after that we may not agree. I believe that your second responsibility is to your family. Your family is your church, and you are the pastor and the assistant pastor of that church. If you fail in your ministry to your family, your other ministries will not have much success either.

Advice to Ministers

This was not an easy lesson for me to learn, and God had to rebuke me several times until it finally got through my thick skull. To me, my responsibility to my members, whom I loved as my own children, came first.

On one occasion, when my wife was sick, I was sitting on the side of her bed, nursing her. The telephone rang, and one of my members was asking me if I could come, that they urgently needed to talk to me about a problem they had. I instinctively jumped up, excused myself, and ran out the door. My wife knew my love for the church and was resigned to my going.

But the Spirit of the Lord spoke to me as soon as I got out the door and said, "I have given you your wife. She is part of your very being. You are to care for her. She needs you more at this moment than others do."

I turned and went back inside. I sat down on the bed and said, "Honey, I decided to stay right here beside you until you get well."

"But what about the phone call?" she asked.

"It was not a matter of life and death," I told her. "They can wait."

My wife's face lit up. Within forty-five minutes she was up and about. "I'm feeling better," she said.

"I would like to eat something. Could you make me some soup?" When I had made the soup, I insisted on feeding it to her. Before long, we started laughing and playing like a couple of kids and having a wonderful time together. My presence did her a world of good.

On other occasions, my wife was not as compliant and was used of the Lord to make me see my error. Once, in the early years of our marriage, my wife said to me, "If your ministry is so important to you that you no longer have time for me, then go ahead with your ministry; but I am going home to my parents. You probably won't miss me anyway."

Boy, that shook me up! How could I minister with a broken home?

On another occasion, in later years, she said to me one day, "You need to stay home today and spend some time with your son. He needs some discipline."

But I had received a call and felt that I needed to make a visit to a member. "Couldn't this wait?" I asked her.

"Well, if you want your son to grow up troubled and rebellious," she told me, "go ahead. If you love your son, stay and deal with him. If that member is more important than the soul of your own son,

Advice to Ministers

then go win them. But you will weep when your own son is lost."

Too many of those who are in the ministry have used their ministry as an excuse to be an irresponsible spouse and an irresponsible parent, and God will not hold them guiltless for that.

I am not suggesting that you resign from your ministry. I am telling you that you must get your priorities right and work on first things first. If you don't have time for your family, you need a total reorganization of your time and how you spend it. Put everything in its proper place.

Why is it that the children of some respected elders are drug addicts? Why is it that the children of some anointed preachers are out in the world walking in sin? These parents are good men and women, but they are confused in their priorities. They have time for any member of the congregation but no time for their own children. And that is simply not right. If you fail in the home, you are a failure. Stop feeding your children the crumbs of life, for they deserve better.

When our ministries become successful, we become very popular, and there are many demands on our time. We are looked up to, pampered, and patted. We enjoy that too much. To our children,

Founded On the Rock

we are just plain *Daddy,* and that hurts our pride. Parenting doesn't seem very important in the light of our other responsibilities, but it is THE MOST IMPORTANT of all our responsibilities.

My wife shocked me when she said: "Darling, what will it profit you if you gain the whole world and lose your own family?" We preachers need to have our preaching turned on us sometimes.

As Christians, we are kings and priests unto God. Every member of the church is a pastor, or an associate pastor, of their own household. Your first congregation is your family. And, if you cannot govern your own home, you cannot discipline your own home, you cannot establish the members of your family in their spiritual foundation, what good can you do for the church? The strength of your congregation depends on the strength of the families who worship there.

One of the pitfalls we face, as workers in the church, is not practicing what we preach. Don't be like those who say, "Do what I say, not what I do." Nothing is worse than a hypocrite.

A priest once told my wife, "We are only holy people from the waist up. From the waist down, we are as normal as anyone else. So, we teach our

Advice to Ministers

congregation how to live right and tell them, 'Do what we tell you. Don't do what we are doing ourselves.' "

One day he made a sermon in the church. He said, "You, who are not married and are living together should separate, because you are living in sin." After the mass, he went into the parish and found his secretary (who was also his girlfriend) packing her suitcase.

"What are you doing, Dear?" he asked.

"I am packing," she replied.

"But why?"

"I can't stay here anymore."

"Why not?"

"Because you just preached to us that those who are living together and are not married are living in sin and should separate."

"No!" he objected, "That is only for the members. It doesn't apply to us." All of us, whether in the ministry or not, must practice what we preach.

Parents are great to tell their children, "Don't do this" and "Don't do that." "DON'T!" "DON'T!" "DON'T!" Children get tired of hearing it. They are so sick of hearing it, in fact, that they want to shout, "Then why are YOU doing it?" "Why are YOU doing it?" "Why are YOU doing it?"

Children don't buy the double standard. What is good for you is also good for them. If it is not wrong for Mama to have a friend in when Daddy is away, then it is not wrong for the children either. We have to practice what we preach.

I read about a man who was an alcoholic. He took his five-year-old son for a walk on the beach, and he carried a can of beer along, sipping as he went. He walked ahead and the son came behind him. He turned to see why his son was behind. "Come on," he said, "What are you doing? "

"I'm coming," the son replied. "I'm following you. I am walking in your footsteps." What a terrible thought that was for the father!

It is true. Your children will follow in your footsteps.

It is wonderful to be involved in the ministry, in any position, to be active in the church in any way. But, please, do nothing at the expense of your family.

If you are a Sunday school teacher and you have children, you have someone to practice the lesson on before Sunday arrives. Teach your children. Give them the lesson first. We spend so much time preparing and teaching others, but we neglect to teach our own.

We go out to pray for others who are sick and believe for their healing miracle. Then, when

Advice to Ministers

someone in our own family gets sick, we turn immediately to medicines and rob them of the privilege of knowing God's power of healing in their lives. Sometimes we don't even offer a prayer for them. This is not right.

If you want your children to learn to pray, let them see the result of prayer in your own home. Don't wait for them to learn it in the church. Let them learn it at home.

If you want your children to have faith, live a life of faith before them. Let your children see firsthand what faith in God can do. There is no better way for them to learn it.

When my son David was four years old, we were living and working in San Francisco. One day he said to me, "Daddy, I need new shoes. These have holes in the bottom."

"Son," I said, "pray that the Lord will give you a new pair."

Two days later, he said to me again, "Daddy, I need new shoes."

I realized that God had put within my power to provide the answer to that boy's prayer. I had the money to buy his shoes, but, I didn't know why, I answered him the same way again: "Pray, son. Ask Jesus to provide your shoes."

Two weeks passed, and David hadn't received his shoes. He came to me rather disgusted and said, "I'm not going to pray anymore for my shoes. Every time I pray, God never answers. And every time I ask you, you just say, 'Pray,' so what's the use? I won't ask you anymore. I will never be a pastor when I grow up because pastors are always poor."

I was left speechless. I went to the Lord in prayer, asking Him to prove to my son that He does answer prayer and that a child could have the experience of receiving an answer to his own prayer, without having everything given to him by his parents.

The next day we were having a telephone evangelism campaign. A brother from Texas was with me. While we were driving along together, he turned to me and asked, "Pastor, would you be offended if I would buy your son a pair of shoes?"

"No," I said, "I won't be offended. He needs new shoes. But, tell me, what made you decide to do it?"

"The Lord spoke to me last night," he said, "and told me to buy your son a pair of shoes."

I told him the size, and he bought two pairs.

When I got home, I called my son and told him, "God has sent a gift for you."

He cried when he saw the shoes and said, "Pastors are not poor, because God is rich." We must

Advice to Ministers

demonstrate what we believe. We must live what we preach. We must exercise what we know.

Even if our children go away from God, they will never forget what they have learned and these experiences will inevitably bring them back.

Christian leaders, our homes should be built *"through wisdom"* and established *"by understanding."* If they are, God has promised that the chambers would be *"filled with all precious and pleasant things."* Prove Him! He never fails. It is time for you, as a Christian leader, to begin setting the example for others by finding God's order for your family.

➜

Chapter 12

Advice to the Unsaved

And they also, if they abide not still in unbelief, shall be grafted in: for God is able to graft them in again. Romans 11:23

Who was before a blasphemer, and a persecutor, and injurious: but I obtained mercy, because I did it ignorantly in unbelief. 1 Timothy 1:13

Many of those who are unsaved have no respect for the authority of the Word of God. They do not, therefore, respond to teachings such as these. They would rather rely on the advice of psychologists and marriage counselors, when it comes to questions of marital and family problems. I understand that, but I also feel that I have a message for these people.

I counsel with many people who are not Christians. They come to me with marital conflicts in various stages. I would much prefer that they realize their need of Christ and be saved, but I counsel with

Advice to the Unsaved

them nevertheless, even if they seem to reject the fact that life can be found only in Jesus.

Some of those with whom I deal are contemplating separation or divorce. And, because those who don't know the Lord also don't know the power of prayer to change things, they often have little or no hope of resolving their conflicts.

I usually ask them this question: "Is this really what you want?" Most of the time, if they are being honest, they will answer that separation or divorce is not really what they want, but they don't see any other alternative.

Ninety-nine percent of those who are suffering the breakup of their marriages don't really want it to happen. They are only proceeding with divorce because they don't know how to mend the marriage. It is not that they don't still love each other. It is not that they don't want to resolve their differences. The problem is that they don't know how to do it.

I recommend to many unbelievers that they go for counseling. If they don't want Christian counseling, even a secular marriage counselor may be able to help them with their basic conflicts. The problem with secular counselors is that the majority of them automatically say, "If you are incompatible, then it is better to split up." They have no fear of God and no respect for His Word or for His power to change the situation of our lives. So, the help they can offer is very limited.

Most of these couples tell me the same story. At the beginning, they love each other. Then, when several years have passed, the relationship begins to sour. It doesn't happen overnight. It happens because of carelessness and slowness to recognize the symptoms of a sick marriage. What they have to do now, I tell them, is to go back to the place where the problems began and face the issues that have divided them.

When you go to a doctor, he will not give you a prescription before he first examines you and diagnoses what the problem is. To complete his diagnosis, he will first ask, "Is there any history of disease in the family?" Then, he will want to know when you first started feeling bad and what the first symptoms were. Then, he will ask how the sickness progressed. He is trying to diagnose your sickness so that he can treat you intelligently.

By diagnosing, frankly and honestly, our marital problems, we can come to many conclusions about what is ailing us. When did this start? What were the first symptoms of trouble? How did this progress? When did this come to a critical point?

Advice to the Unsaved

"Once we were lovey-dovey, but now we fight like cats and dogs," some say. What happened to them?

The problem is never that there is no more love for one another. That is one of the symptoms of the problem, not the problem itself. Heal the sickness, and the love will return. People say, "I just don't love her anymore." So what? You *can* love her, and you can love her more than before.

When a person is sick, they often lose their appetite. But the doctor doesn't say, "Oh yes, you have Loss Of Appetite Sickness." There is no such sickness. Loss of appetite is a result of some other sickness. Cure the sickness, and the natural appetite will return. Cure the basic ills in your marriage, and the love will return.

"I have no more love for my husband." Maybe not, but you *can* have. The love is there, but it is suppressed by some aggravation of life. Anger and resentment will quench your feeling of love. You might conclude, "All the love is gone out of our marriage." Maybe so, but, if you let God heal your marriage, all that love will come rushing back. You will see.

Love is not based upon what you feel at the moment. It is not based on the circumstances of the moment. Just because you feel good doesn't mean you are in love, and just because you feel bad doesn't mean you are out of love. Forget about how your feel.

When you are excited and feel arousal that doesn't mean you are in love, and just because you are not feeling excitement and arousal now doesn't mean that you are out of love. Love is not based on feelings. We have it backwards. Feelings must be based on love.

So the first thing I would ask unbelievers to do is to realize that they still love each other and don't really want to separate. Then, they must be convinced that God will help them resolve their difficulties. If not, they are wasting my time and theirs too.

The second thing I say to the unsaved goes something like this: "Are you willing to just throw away all those years of sacrifice and commitment and life together? What a terrible waste! Your investment in this marriage is great. You have put a lot into this. Will you now just throw all that investment to the wind? Will you just dump your life to this point in the trash can?" No one likes to lose their investment, and surely this must make some think twice about what they are doing.

I consider this very provocative question to

Advice to the Unsaved

be a good one for everyone, believers as well as nonbelievers, and it usually brings a very positive response. Often, at this point, I am able to convince unbelieving couples to give God a chance in their lives and to lead them to the love of Jesus. If they are willing to accept new life in Christ, their other problems suddenly seem very small and surmountable. God heals relationships. God heals broken hearts. God restores broken marriages. Get God, and you will be on the track to recovery in your marriage.

I have an interesting little exercise that I use in premarital counseling and also with couples in trouble. I tell them: "Take two pieces of paper: on the one, write down all the good and positive qualities of your mate. On the other one, write down all the things you don't like about your mate."

If they find that they have written down a lot of negative things about their mate, I ask them to accept it as a challenge to help their mate overcome those negatives and be the best person he or she can be.

If the two have a fairly good relationship with each other (as in premarital counseling), I suggest that they show each other what they have written. That gives them some goals to work toward, some matters to take before the Lord in serious prayer. We even discuss them together.

If the relationship is not strong (as in the cases of marriages in trouble), I ask them to keep these pieces of paper as a prayer list, to believe God for one item at a time, then to cross off any negative points that improve and add them to the positive side. In that way, they can see the hand of God at work in their affairs.

When a husband is praying for his wife, and a wife is praying for her husband, there will be no time to fight.

I also ask those who come for counseling to read together the Book of Proverbs. You might try it also. It is full of gems of wisdom that will make you strong.

If you are an unbeliever and are reading this book, realize that you need God's help in finding His order for your family. ¢

Chapter 13

Advice to Believers Who Have Unsaved Spouses

And the woman which hath an husband that believeth not, and if he be pleased to dwell with her, let her not leave him. For the unbelieving husband is sanctified by the wife, and the unbelieving wife is sanctified by the husband: else were your children unclean; but now are they holy. But if the unbelieving depart, let him depart. A brother or a sister is not under bondage in such cases: but God hath called us to peace.

1 Corinthians 7:13-15

Those individuals who have unbelieving spouses must, first of all, recognize that their commitment to marriage is for life and doesn't change just because their chosen partner fails to agree with them in matters of faith. The Scriptures declare:

Founded On the Rock

> *Wherefore they are no more twain, but one flesh. What therefore God hath joined together, let not man put asunder.* Matthew 19:6

As a believer, your first responsibility is to God, and He would not want you to deny Him for the sake of keeping peace in your marriage. But you also cannot abandon your family because of differences in opinion, even in this crucial matter. Marriage is a commitment for life, come what may.

A believer who has an unsaved spouse faces unusual problems that most of us can only imagine. He or she loves the Lord and wants to be true to Him. At the same time, he or she loves his or her spouse and wants to be a good mate and, through a life of testimony, win that unsaved mate to the Lord. These may seem to be mutually incompatible goals, but it need not be so. God's order for marriage is unchangeable, regardless of the faith of one's mate. Christian or not, His standard for family life is the same.

Men, just because your wife is not a believer, don't love her any less. You have been joined to her by God and are *"one flesh"* with her. Let your love reach out to her and, eventually, be the catalyst of her coming to Christ.

Advice to Believers Who Have Unsaved Spouses

Woman, even though your husband is not a believer, don't reject him as head of your household. Submit to him — within the framework of God's Word and within the boundaries of morality.

Some Christian traditions in this regard are not biblically founded. For instance, some feel that a woman with an unsaved husband has no right to testify in public or to do anything else for the Lord, but this is not true. Our relationship with Christ is a very personal thing. If a woman loves God, she has every right to speak of that love — even though her husband might not agree. Every individual has to make up his or her own mind in the matter of faith. What a husband does or does not do cannot be blamed on the wife or vice versa.

The fact that her husband doesn't attend church services should not keep a woman from sharing her experience. Her commitment to the Lord cannot be measured by what someone else does or does not do. When God has blessed you, how can you be silent — no matter what others do?

If the husband is happy for his wife to go out and conduct Bible studies or to do some other work for the Lord, I don't see any problem. She must be sure to maintain her house well, prepare the meals, and keep her other family obligations. If she keeps all her commitments to her husband and children, there is nothing preventing her from working for the Lord.

If your husband is unsaved, take advantage of every opportunity he gives you and, as you do, believe God continually to change your husband's heart so that he, too, might love the Lord and desire to do God's will. Most unsaved husbands will not prohibit their wives from attending church and doing things for the Lord — as long as the wife is keeping her house well and caring faithfully for her children.

If I were an unbeliever, and my wife was attending many church services, but when I went home, the bed was not made, the house was dirty, the clothes were not washed, and the food was not cooked, then I would be unhappy. That is understandable. Even a Christian man would not feel happy in those circumstances.

You must set your priorities, and, if you have a big family, your first responsibility is to them. If you have no children at home, if there are only the two of you, it is much easier to cope with the household chores, and you can have more time to dedicate to the things of the Lord.

A Christian woman must never neglect her children for whatever reason. Building strong relationships with them takes time and effort.

Advice to Believers Who Have Unsaved Spouses

Christian women whose husbands are unbelievers have extra duties. They must take on the role of priest of the family. Many times their husbands are not aware of their responsibilities in giving direction to the family, of teaching and of discipline. It is possible that the woman will have to "take up the slack" in all of these areas.

Some Christian women, as a result, are overworked and need help in organizing their home schedule. Time, to them, is even more precious and must be used well. They need to let their family know exactly what is expected of them and make sure that every member sticks to the schedule.

But the life of the Christian woman with an unbeliever for a husband or a Christian man with an unbelieving wife is not impossible. Many have set the example by carrying on very well under these difficult circumstances, and you can do it too. Be *"the light"* that shines before that unsaved one, revealing the glory of Christ that will attract them to Him. Be *"the salt"* that will preserve your family so that the various members will not be devoured by the enemy. Let them be *"sanctified"* through your diligence to faith.

Accept the challenge and believe God to help you begin finding God's order for your family. →

Part V

The Conclusion

Chapter 14

The Power of Prayer to Change Your Situation and My Prayer for You

And all things, whatsoever ye shall ask in prayer, believing, ye shall receive.   Matthew 21:22

Prayer works wonders. Prayer can change any situation. Never minimize or underestimate the power of prayer. There is nothing that prayer cannot do. When you pray believing, God will perform His Word.

If Christians would pray for the living like the Catholics in our country pray for the dead, we would all be blessed. They meet together and pray for nine nights after the death of a loved one. But they continue praying for another forty days. Then, every year, they celebrate the anniversary of the death of their loved one with more prayers. I think there are more prayers offered for the dead than for the living.

When we will pray and appropriate into our daily lives the provision of God's Word, practicing what God's Word teaches us, it is not difficult to maintain unity in the home or to maintain a sweet spirit. It is not difficult to have more love for each other. Nothing is impossible with God.

When disagreements arise, the husband is sure that his wife is wrong and must change. The wife, however, is equally sure that her husband is wrong and that he must change.

I find that it is usually me that needs to change; and, if I change, the situation will change too. When we pray, God can answer in one of three ways:

1. God can change the situation.
2. God can change your spouse.
3. God can change you.

Ninety percent of the time it is neither the situation or your spouse that God wants to change, but you. Because of that fact, many Christians don't want to submit their marital problems to prayer. They are afraid that God will change them, and they don't want to be changed. We always want the other person to change. But change doesn't come until I change. And, when I change, everything changes.

The Power of Prayer to Change Your Situation and My Prayer for You

I believe in the power of prayer, and I want to pray with you now. If you will sincerely open your heart to God and pray with me, God will hear and answer our plea and give you victory in your marriage and in your home today.

If you are near your spouse, take him or her by the hand as we pray together. There is a remedy. It is not too late. The Holy Spirit can change your lives. If your children are near, gather them around and pray together with them.

Let us pray:

God Almighty,

Let Your anointing flow through this couple. In the name of Jesus, let the spirit of unity come to their marriage, for a healthy relationship in total agreement. Bind them together in the love of God, and may the Holy Spirit take complete control and dominion over their affairs. Help them to set their marriage in order.

Jesus, embrace them with Your love and grace and reinforce the unity, the agreement, the love, the fellowship, the relationship with one another. In the name of Jesus Christ, join their hearts together and make them one in the power of the Holy Spirit.

Thank You for this family that is represented. May the power of the Holy Spirit bind the individual members together in unity and harmony and love. Oh God, establish them. Make them strong in the Kingdom of God and in the things of the Lord. Help them to set their house in order and to build their home upon a solid foundation, the foundation of the Word of God.

I pray that You will help the children to be willing to submit to the authority of their parents. May every rebellious spirit be broken. Break down all stubbornness and defiance. We come against the spirit of our age, in the liberating name of Jesus of Nazareth. Give these children the ability to respond in a positive way to the God-given authority entrusted to their parents.

May parents have a new love for their children. Let their rulership be conducted with much tenderness and caring. Help them to exercise their authority well to the glory of God.

Now, let us be glad and rejoice and give glory to God. Let us thank Him for the privilege of being Christians, of knowing personally the God of the

Universe, whose grace is sufficient for every trial. His love is abundant, and His provision is without limit.

I want you to thank God for your spouse. Thank God for your children. Children, thank God for your parents. Be happy in the Lord. Rejoice in the Lord our God, and bless His wonderful name.

I believe that God has heard our prayer and has enlarged our thinking; I believe He has enlarged our hearts; I believe He has enlarged the boundary of our vision.

It is God's will to heal our families. It is His will to bless and prosper our homes. Beloved, present yourself as a living sacrifice to God, a reasonable service. Mom, Dad, children, present yourself now as a living sacrifice to God.

Husband, accept your position as the priest of your household. Put your arms around your children and your wife and pray for them, lift them into the presence of Almighty God in faith. Believe for their safety. Believe for their prosperity. Believe God's promises for them.

Children, ask your parents to forgive you for your rebellious attitude. Tell them you love them.

Parents, ask your children to forgive you for not governing in love.

Now, Lord, bring healing to these families. Bring wholeness to these households, I pray. Let the barriers between parents and children be removed. And let there be a new love between every member of the family.

Now, put your arms around your spouse and give him or her a warm kiss, not because you have to, but because you want to. Do it in the name of Jesus and for the glory of God, the Father.

I say to you now:

Be whole! In the name of Jesus.
Be set free from hindrances!
Receive the healing of your family!

In the name of Jesus Christ,
Amen!

Contact Information

Pastor Ray Llarena
Global Evangelistic Ministries
P O Box 850
Bloomingdale, IL 60108

bishopray1@yahoo.com

www.ingramcontent.com/pod-product-compliance
Lightning Source LLC
Chambersburg PA
BHW032110090426
CB00007B/298